THE SCOTS IRISH
OF EARLY PENNSYLVANIA

T0167865

JUDITH RIDNER

THE SCOTS IRISH of

EARLY PENNSYLVANIA

A VARIED PEOPLE

TEMPLE UNIVERSITY PRESS
Philadelphia • Rome • Tokyo

TEMPLE UNIVERSITY PRESS
Philadelphia, Pennsylvania 19122
www.temple.edu/tempress

Published by Temple University Press in partnership with The Pennsylvania
Historical Association

Library of Congress Cataloging-in-Publication Data

Names: Ridner, Judith A., author.
Title: The Scots Irish of early Pennsylvania : a varied people / Judith
Ridner.
Description: Philadelphia : Temple University Press, 2018. | Series: In the
Pennsylvania history series | Includes bibliographical references and index.
Identifiers: LCCN 2017053971 (print) | LCCN 2017061772 (ebook) |
ISBN 9781932304312 (E-book) | ISBN 9781932304329 (pbk. : alk. paper)
Subjects: LCSH: Scots-Irish—Pennsylvania—History—17th century. |
Scots-Irish—Pennsylvania—History—18th century. | Pennsylvania—
History—Colonial period, ca. 1600–1775. | Pennsylvania—History—
Revolution, 1775–1783.
Classification: LCC F160.S4 (ebook) | LCC F160.S4 R53 2018 (print) |
DDC 974.8/02—dc23
LC record available at https://lccn.loc.gov/2017053971

Design by Kate Nichols

9 8 7 6

CONTENTS

EDITORS' FOREWORD

ON BEHALF OF THE MEMBERS AND OFFICERS of the Pennsylvania Historical Association (PHA), we are delighted to present the second book in the newly redesigned *Pennsylvania History Series* (*PHS*). The *PHS* mission remains to provide timely, relevant, high-quality scholarship in a compact and accessible form. Produced by and for scholars engaged in the teaching of Pennsylvania history, books in the series are aimed at students and are intended for use in the classroom and broader public history settings. Our partnership with Temple University Press brings the expertise and resources of a respected academic publisher to a book series that has been in existence since the late 1940s and includes more than thirty titles.

Judith Ridner has enriched our series greatly with her important work on the Scots Irish in Pennsylvania. She offers an engaging narrative that sheds light on the complex identity of the members of this group and their importance in the state's history. A key component of this identity is their Presbyterian faith, and the discussion of this aspect of Scots Irish life in the New World will prove valuable to those who are interested in American religious and social history. The character sketches that Ridner includes illustrate the class differences among the settlers and allow her to explore the premise that the Scots Irish were a varied people. Ultimately, she demonstrates the importance of the Scots Irish in the development of early U.S. society and the legacy of the Scots Irish that lives on today.

We thank Judith Ridner for providing us with an exceptionally engaging and well-written manuscript. In addition, we thank our peer reviewers for

offering suggestions that strengthened an already excellent work, and we grate-
fully acknowledge the assistance of our editorial board and our PHA *Pennsylvania History Series* predecessors—particularly Diane Wenger, whose efforts
during a difficult time kept the series alive and set the stage for its current revival. We are also grateful to Brenda Kern of Waveline Direct, LLC, for de-
signing the series logo and to Vicky Simmel of Gannon Associates Insurance
for her efforts on our behalf. Finally, we owe a debt of gratitude to our partners
at Temple University Press for agreeing to take on this series.

—ALLEN DIETERICH-WARD, Shippensburg University

—BEVERLY C. TOMEK, University of Houston, Victoria

PENNSYLVANIA HISTORY SERIES EDITORIAL BOARD

JANET LINDMAN, Rowan University

CURT MINER, Pennsylvania Historical and Museum Commission

TRACY NEUMANN, Wayne State University

DONNA RILLING, Stony Brook University

ANNE ROSE, Pennsylvania State University

DANIEL SIDORICK, Rutgers University, New Brunswick

ACKNOWLEDGMENTS

WRITING A BOOK is never an easy or isolated task. Although the process of research and writing can be fascinating and rewarding, as it was for this book, it is always more challenging and time-consuming than expected. It also depends heavily on the advice and assistance of librarians and archivists, readers and editors for the publisher, and family members and friends. Thus, as I bring this project to a close, I extend my warmest and sincerest thanks to all the people and institutions that helped me along the way.

In particular, I thank the former *Pennsylvania History Series* editor Diane Wenger for inviting me to tackle this project. I thank Beverly C. Tomek and Allen Dieterich-Ward, the current series editors, for their help and patience in seeing this book to completion; they were always there to answer my questions and to give me the gentle prods I needed to keep the project moving forward. The manuscript also benefited enormously from the careful assessment of two anonymous readers for Temple University Press, who offered their (much appreciated) enthusiastic support of my work and provided some great leads for me to pursue; their insights have certainly made this a better book. Finally, I owe special thanks to the geographer Scott Drzyzga at Shippensburg University, who took time out of his own busy schedule to create the maps for this book.

On a more personal note, I thank Peter Messer, my husband and a first-rate historian, for serving as the chief sounding board for my ideas and interpretations. As the best-read historian I know, Peter is a constant source of knowledge, inspiration, and companionship. I thank him for being there during the highs and the lows of life, which have included a lot of travel, a couple of major moves, and many bicycle rides, hikes, and dog walks. Last but not least, I acknowledge my "new" Irish family, the McGees. For me, an adoptee who had long been told that she was the daughter of two Irish immigrants who had made their way to New York City in the 1960s, Ireland has always loomed large and has shaped the people and places I have chosen to study as a historian. Still, with my German surname, my personal Irish identity always remained obscured from public view. That changed several months ago, during the final stages of manuscript preparation, when an AncestryDNA match to a cousin in Ireland led to the discovery of my birth father, his brother, and three half siblings. In the short time I have known them, I have learned much about the family's history (the family's name was associated long ago with County Antrim in Ulster), the Ireland that they came from (one of the counties bordering Ulster), and their experiences as Irish Catholic newcomers in America. I dedicate this book to them—Noel, Mary, Joe, Deb, Colleen, and Rory—in the hope that our relationship will continue to grow and that I will succeed in proving to Joe that early Protestant Irish immigrants were not all savages.

THE SCOTS IRISH
OF EARLY PENNSYLVANIA

INTRODUCTION

Defining These Varied People

WHO ARE THE SCOTS IRISH? The answer seems simple: the Scots Irish were one of the largest non-English immigrant groups in eighteenth-century America. These Scots Protestants (mostly Lowlanders and Presbyterians) were the quintessential "peoples in motion" of the early modern Europe.[1] Encouraged by the English to relocate to Ireland's northern province of Ulster, they had migrated across the Irish Sea during the late seventeenth and early eighteenth centuries to "plant" themselves as a Protestant colonizing force among Ireland's native Roman Catholics. Later in the eighteenth century, when economic, political, and religious conditions in Ulster turned against them and their interests, large numbers of these Scots Protestants (estimates suggest about 250,000 people before 1815) uprooted themselves again and migrated across the Atlantic to the American colonies, particularly to Pennsylvania.[2]

Still, when we think of the Scots Irish, as they came to be known in America, we imagine not a Pennsylvanian but a southerner and, most often, one man, Andrew Jackson. Jackson, the seventh president of the United States, was the son of Scots Irish immigrant parents who left Ulster in 1765 and settled in the Carolina backcountry (probably by way of Philadelphia), where Jackson was born two years later. Nicknamed "Old Hickory" for his toughness on the battlefield, Jackson earned respect and fame as a Tennessee planter, merchant, and slaveholder, a ruthless soldier, and a formidable political leader of the nascent Democratic Party. Since his own time, he has epitomized popular portrayals of the Scots Irish as a hardy, vigorous, and assertive "breed" who were "born fighters" and who became America's prototypical backcountry pioneers.[3]

This popular image of Andrew Jackson, published near the time of his death in 1845, portrays him as a "hero," "sage," and "patriot." (N. Currier. *General Andrew Jackson. The Hero, the Sage and the Patriot,* ca. 1845. New York: Published by N. Currier. Lithograph, hand-colored. LC-USZ62–2343, Library of Congress, Prints and Photographs Division, Washington, D.C.)

Historians have long argued that the Scots Irish arrived in America desperately poor, with only the democratic principles of their Presbyterian religion to anchor them. Led by men who were armed with axes and rifles and who carried quarts of whiskey to fire and soothe their tempers, these families, whose female members remained mostly in the shadows, hacked their farms out of the wilderness and then fiercely defended their claims by fighting Indian and British enemies. Their popular image, epitomized by Jackson, is that of a strong, courageous, and masculine people who embodied the core American values of patriotism, pragmatism, and individualism and a willingness to defend those values with a fight.[4] With Jackson as a symbol of their rise from rags to riches and power, the Scots Irish not only assimilated to America; they assumed mythic proportions as an American success story. Today, because their "traits . . . grew into a national identity generalized across the cultural landscape," they remain emblems of American identity; America, in sum, became more like them.[5]

Alongside this mythic image, however, is a competing, derogatory image of the Scots Irish as "rednecks" or "hillbillies." The setting is still the American backcountry stretching from Pennsylvania south to the Carolinas and Georgia. Yet this group portrait of men, women, and children is fuzzier than that of Jackson because the Scots Irish settlers in it are anonymous, and the log house behind them is long demolished. Also unlike Jackson, whose proud, upright stance and formal dress express his power and status as a man, these settlers are defined by their disadvantages. As their log dwelling, simple clothing, and humble surroundings suggest, these people suffered from poverty and cultural isolation.

Today, in our polarized political climate, group portraits like this one elicit divergent responses. Some might look on it empathetically because they have some historical understanding of how tough frontier life could be, or because they identify with the conservative politics of today's undereducated, underemployed, and impoverished rural white working class. Others might be more judgmental, labeling these modern-day Scots Irish as "hillbillies" whose intolerance of immigrants and pessimistic view of the United States, born of their anger over their declining economic opportunities and their general fear of the future, helped elect Donald Trump as president of the

This 1933 photograph of a farm family in Missouri epitomizes popular images of the hardscrabble existence endured by many rural Americans, particularly the Scots Irish. (Historic American Buildings Survey. *Watts Log Cabin, Grandad Spring, Gravois Mills, Morgan County, MO, 1933.* Photograph. Library of Congress, Washington, D.C., https://www.loc.gov/item/mo0823/.)

United States.[6] These negative assessments echo many of the similarly harsh assessments offered by observers in the past. Earlier critics pointed to the hillbilly image as confirmation that the Scots Irish were a separate and inferior "breed" whose members lived in poverty because their men were quarrelsome and hot-tempered and lacked the industriousness and sobriety to prosper in America, and their women were burdened by continual childbearing and nursing and years of child rearing. These people were the "sordid refuse" of America; their story was a cautionary tale.[7]

The persistence of these sharply contrasting and heavily stereotyped images of the Scots Irish suggests that this group defies easy description or categorization. But why is that so? The negative reactions to them seem puzzling, given their privileged status as white people who spoke English and were committed Protestants. What was it about this early immigrant group that makes them such slippery historical subjects?

To begin, there is considerable confusion about what to call them. They have so many names that one historian calls them the "people with no name."[8] In early modern Ireland, these Scots Presbyterian settlers were often called "Ulster Scots," "northern Scots," or "northern dissenters." Once in colonial Pennsylvania, where Irish Catholics were few in number until the nineteenth century, most of their Anglo-American contemporaries referred to them simply as "Irish," a designation that acknowledged the Irish cultural identity (likely exemplified by their Irish-style brogue) that many had acquired in Ulster. The hyphenated term "Scotch-Irish," which is by far the most popular name used to describe them, did not come into wide use until the nineteenth century when American Irish Protestants used the label to distance themselves from the waves of Irish Catholic immigrants who began entering U.S. ports after 1815, and especially during the famine era of the 1840s and 1850s.

The term had more ambiguous connotations in the eighteenth century, when the most privileged of Pennsylvania's Scots Irish colonists—those who remained mostly in and near Philadelphia—perceived "Scotch-Irish" as a derogatory label; they preferred to call themselves "Irish," or "Irish Presbyterians," signifying their geographic origins within the margins of Britain's empire and their religious identity as stalwart, though dissenting, Protestants. Scots Irish colonists of humbler economic means, however, especially male heads of household who lived in the colony's turbulent backcountry of the 1760s, referred to themselves explicitly and proudly as "Scotch-Irish." For them, this name was a way to separate their interests from those of other, competing groups—Scots, Irish (mostly Quaker), Germans, and Indians— who lived around them in the backcountry and to lay claim to a distinct political identity in the colony.[9]

Today, although "Scotch-Irish" is perceived by some as a pejorative term—since scotch is the name of a whiskey rather than a people—it is still used by many of the descendants of the early settlers and continues to appear in much of the popular literature written about them. Scholars, by contrast, have for the most part adopted "Scots Irish" (the term used in this volume), "Ulster Irish," or "Ulster Presbyterians" as the preferred names for this ethnic group. Although these terms are imprecise in their own way too, scholars favor them because they capture the group's culturally hybrid status, including their Scots ethnic heritage and residency in Ireland, their geographic concentration in Ulster, and their standing as dissenting Protestants, which distinguished them from others in Britain's Atlantic World.

Why should we care that the Scots Irish have so many names? Names express identities, and for the members of an ethnic group, their name points to their distinctiveness as a people. The profusion of names given to and used by the Scots Irish reflects an identity that varied according to the different geographical and cultural contexts in which they lived. Mobility from one cultural borderland to another within the British Empire defined much of the Scots Irish experience. Over the course of two centuries, they moved from Scotland to Ireland and from Ireland to America. Once in America, they moved from Philadelphia and New Castle west into the Pennsylvania backcountry and the Midwest, and south into Virginia, the Carolinas, and Georgia. In each place, they lived among others who were sometimes hostile to their presence. In Ireland, they lived among Catholic Irish and English; in America, they lived among many other European ethnic groups, Indians, and even some Africans. Surviving and even prospering in each of these cultural circumstances demanded adaptability.

The Scots Irish were also a highly diverse group of migrants that included men and women of varying class backgrounds and economic interests. Having a flexible sense of who they were as people allowed them to accommodate their differences. Many of them had sufficient economic means to immigrate to Pennsylvania as free people, often traveling in families. With education and connections on their side, these men became traders, merchants, and professionals in Philadelphia or in interior towns such as Carlisle; they were farmers, millers, and rural landowners; some even rose to power as military and political leaders during the American Revolution and the early national period; they also became the founding patriarchs of long-lasting Irish American families. Their wives bore, reared, and educated their children; many also helped advance their family's economic fortunes by engaging in various domestic manufacturing enterprises, such as spinning or dairying, or by acting as "deputy husbands" who ran family farms or businesses during a spouse's absence.

A large segment of those who left Ireland, however, did not possess such advantages; these Scots Irish immigrants came to Pennsylvania as indentured servants, traveling alone, rather than in family groups. When freed, these men and women, who typically remained single during their time of service and are mostly anonymous to us today, often became mired in poverty, existing on the margins of Pennsylvania society. Women had a tougher time than men. In the patriarchal world of eighteenth-century America, those women who remained single were the most vulnerable; it was not unusual for them to end up in one of Philadelphia's poor houses. Men had more options. It was easier for even the poorest among them to keep moving as they worked to build families, find land, and define their place in America. Although these men and their families remain mostly forgotten to us today, their pursuit of opportunity played a fundamental role in extending Pennsylvania's—and America's—frontier and displacing its native peoples, often violently.[10]

Through it all and regardless of their class standing stood their religion. Although the Scots Irish diverged many times in how they expressed their Calvinist beliefs, Presbyterianism held them together, anchoring their cultural lives as a diverse and mobile people of the borderlands.

———————

THIS BOOK TELLS THE STORY of these Scots Irish migrants and their experiences in early Pennsylvania. As such, it offers a much-overdue synthesis and reassessment of a critical chapter of their history in the United States.[11] Its chronological concentration is on the "long" eighteenth century, the era stretching from approximately 1700 to 1820, which marked the heyday of the Scots Irish. During this time they emigrated in large numbers from Ireland and played pivotal roles in the settlement and development of America. The book's geographic focus is on Pennsylvania, the colony and state where the Scot Irish made their first American home and where many of the developments that would define them as an ethnic group in America took place.

1

LIFE IN ULSTER

I finding this opportunity have made this my messenger to acquaint you of ye miserable condition that I have brought myself and my family to in staying on your honor's land these years past. (Alexander Crawford, County Donegal, Ireland, to Alexander Murray, his Scottish landlord, July 1736)[1]

This Kingdom is much worse than it was even when you left it; Trading of all sorts and in all Branches [is] Growing worse; and every day opens a new prospect of woe & misery. (Henry Johnston, County Down, Ireland, to his brother, Moses Johnston, in Lancaster County, Pennsylvania, April 1773)[2]

ALEXANDER CRAWFORD and Henry Johnston exemplify the diversity of Scots Presbyterian society in eighteenth-century Ulster. Crawford was a semi-literate tenant farmer who probably grew grain, pastured livestock, and fished for subsistence. He lived in rural Donegal, Ulster's westernmost county along the Atlantic seacoast, on twenty acres of land he rented from Alexander Murray, an absentee landlord in Scotland. Johnston, by contrast, was a town dweller in the easternmost Ulster county of Down, where he farmed a bit and wove linen. He was better educated than Crawford and may have worked as a schoolmaster sometime in the past.[3]

Despite the geographic distance, personal circumstances, and nearly forty years that separated them, Crawford and Johnston had important experiences in common. Both men were Presbyterians whose Scots ancestors had immigrated to Ireland during the seventeenth century in search of opportunity and advancement. Yet, as their statements suggest, circumstances had changed by the eighteenth century, and they shared a growing sense of disillusionment over the economically inhospitable place Ireland had become for Scots Presbyterians like themselves. Whether living in western or eastern Ulster, in a rural area or a city, subsisting as a tenant farmer or a linen weaver, they felt the squeeze of Ireland's shifting and contracting economy, which intensified as the century progressed. Economic hardship was compounded by newly instituted religious and political restrictions that further constricted the freedom and authority of Ulster's Scots Presbyterians. Ireland was no longer a place of opportunity and hope but one of challenges and difficulties where hard-working Scots Presbyterians like Crawford and Johnston found it increasingly difficult to survive.

This chapter explains how and why eighteenth-century Ireland became a less hospitable place for Scots Presbyterian settlers of Ulster such as Crawford, Johnston, and their families. It discusses the history of Scots Presbyterian migration to Ireland beginning in the seventeenth century and details how British policies intent on colonizing Ireland reconfigured Ulster's economic, political, and social worlds in ways that drove many Scots settlers to immigrate to America by the eighteenth century.

Origins of the Ulster Plantation

Ulster's Scots Presbyterians, including families such as Crawford's and Johnston's, traced their roots to England's Elizabethan-era conquest of Ireland. Beginning in the late twelfth century, England's Anglo-Norman ruling class had tried to conquer and control Ireland and its Gaelic natives. These takeover attempts, however, saw only mixed success. The first Anglo-Norman invaders to Ireland were vastly outnumbered, and they responded by adapting to the Gaelic society around them. Over several centuries, these "Old English" settlers (descendants of the invading Anglo-Normans) became cultural hybrids; they married into various Irish clan families and adopted Gaelic culture, language, and law but remained connected to English commercial networks. This adaptation severely compromised English control of Ireland so that by 1500, although parts of Ireland enjoyed a close trade relationship with England, England's cultural and political authority over the island was confined mostly to Dublin and its hinterlands in a defended area known as the English Pale. "Beyond the Pale" in the rest of Ireland, the English Crown relied on the goodwill and economic interests of the Old English settlers to maintain order among the country's powerful Gaelic lords and the large majority of poor, Gaelic peasants.[4]

Despite such complications, England never abandoned its plans to conquer Ireland. During the reign of the Tudors (1485–1603), and particularly after the English Reformation (1534) and the founding of the Church of England (Anglican Church), England took a new and deeper interest in subduing Catholic Ireland. The birth and growth of English Protestantism boosted an increasingly militant and ethnocentric English nationalism that Queen Elizabeth I (reign 1558–1603) channeled into more aggressive expansionism in Ireland and the Americas. To justify their policies, the Tudors "recast" Ireland as "a savage land" that was occupied by a people who were, one English soldier wrote, "more uncivil, more uncleanly, more barbarous, and more brutish . . . than any other part of the world that is known."[5] With English military forces on the rise in Ireland, England's army met any resistance or disloyalty from Old English elites or Gaelic lords with violence followed by confiscations of land and other punitive legal-political policies aimed at destabilizing the authority of these ruling elites. But warfare was costly, especially at a time when England was in hot competition with Catholic Spain and Crown resources were often insufficient to meet the demands of a growing state. To conquer Ireland, England needed more cost-effective strategies that would better control its native inhabitants while simultaneously harnessing its economic resources for England's, and particularly the Crown's, benefit.[6]

The answer was the establishment of plantations. The English would pacify Ireland and its wild Roman Catholic inhabitants by colonizing it with Protestant settlers who would "bring the island closer in character to England."[7] First in the eastern and southern Irish provinces of Leinster and Munster in the 1560s, and then in Ulster in the 1570s, England offered confiscated estates on favorable terms to mostly English and some Scots Protestant landlords, whom they called undertakers (meaning one who undertakes to plant settlers), and their tenants whose Protestantism would ensure their loyalty to the English Crown.[8] The English had high hopes for these settlers. Aside from securing English cultural and political authority, they would remake Ireland's landscape by replacing pastoralism with agriculture and commerce that would better exploit the country's natural resources; they would also build a more permanent urban infrastructure of towns and roads and transplant a stratified and diverse, English-style occupational structure to Ireland. The goal was to improve what the English perceived as a "neglected land."[9] Yet these first plantation efforts met with violent resistance from Ireland's Gaelic lords and Catholic peasantry. Consequently, much like the Old English before them, Ireland's sixteenth-century Protestant settlers

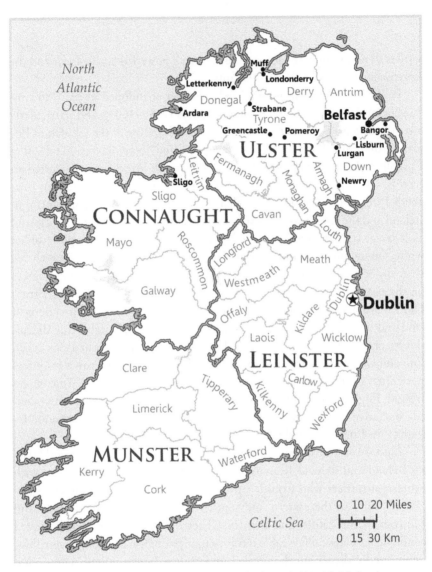

This map of Ireland shows provinces, counties, and selected cities. Highlighted are selected port cities and some of the Ulster place names shared by towns or townships in Pennsylvania (for Ulster place names in Pennsylvania, see the map featured in the Conclusion). (Map by Scott Drzyzga.)

were vastly outnumbered by hostile Catholic natives, and many of them left in response. England's first experiment with plantations ended in failure.[10]

Success came, however, after the English victory in the Nine Years' War of 1594 to 1603 (a war of resistance against English authority by Gaelic lords in Ulster), and the larger, more ambitious, and Scots-dominated Ulster plantations of the seventeenth century.[11] These settlements, which have left a legacy of towns, crumbling defensive walls, castle and manor house ruins, and sectarian tensions in modern Ulster, were founded during the reign of King James I (1603–1625), the first of the Scottish Stuart family monarchs whose ascendency united the thrones of Scotland and England (James, the son of Mary, Queen of Scots, reigned simultaneously as James VI of Scotland from 1567 to 1625). As the center of resistance, Ulster had been the most recalcitrant province during the war, and James hoped to subdue it by winning the loyalty of its recently defeated Gaelic lords by granting them English noble titles and continued control of their lands. But his plans did not work. The province's Gaelic leaders fled to the Continent in what is called the "Flight of the Earls" in 1607, and six of nine Ulster counties they controlled were forfeited to the Crown. These lands were the basis for England's new and more enduring plantation project, which began in Ulster during the 1610s.[12]

More critical to the history of the Scots Irish, James I also made a point of attracting Scots Protestants settlers to his Ulster plantations. Scots involvement made sense. The proximity of the western coast of Scotland to the eastern tip of Ulster ensured that immigration by Scots would be ongoing and dynamic. Because Ulster's climate was similar to Scotland's, agricultural practices were easily transferable. Ancient Gaelic cultural ties also linked some western Scots, particularly the inhabitants of its western isles, to Ulster's Gaelic Irish. King James I had obvious affinities for his fellow Scots, whose "middle temper" between "English tender" sensibilities and "Irish rude breeding," he thought particularly well suited to this enterprise.[13] Many in England were thus optimistic that these loyal, Protestant Scots settlers might accomplish what others before them had not by planting a civilization that would overwhelm and finally subdue what was perceived as the savage culture of Ireland's Catholic natives. Such expectations were well founded. Ulster, according to one historian, was "the despair of the Tudors," but it "became the stronghold of the Irish protestant interest and the British connection under the Stuarts" largely because of the Scots who came to Ireland in great numbers during the seventeenth century.[14]

The Scots Come to Ulster

The Scots were a highly mobile people in the early modern world, and Ulster was one of their principal destinations. Scottish migration to northern Ireland happened in two major waves. The first migration of approximately twenty thousand to thirty thousand Scots took place between 1609 and 1640 and was inspired by King James's plantation scheme. These families settled mostly in the eastern Ulster counties of Antrim and Down, which were closest to Scotland.[15] Then, migration mostly halted for two decades during the upheavals of the War of the Three Kingdoms, a series of civil wars in England, Scotland, and Ireland between 1639 and 1651 during which multiple insurgent groups rose to challenge royal, English, or Protestant authority.[16] The Irish manifestation of these wars, the Irish Rising or Rebellion of 1641, which began when some of Ulster's remaining Catholic earls launched an insurrection aimed at reforming Ireland's governance and protecting their interests, sparked an island-wide, anti-English, anti-Protestant rising among the country's Irish Catholic peasantry. During this war, which lasted for ten years, Catholics targeted Ireland's Protestant government and settlers, including Scots settlers in Ulster. The English fought back brutally, aided in part by an army of some ten thousand Scottish soldiers who arrived in 1642 to protect their Protestant kinsmen in Ulster. With the 1649 invasion by the English Puritan leader Oliver Cromwell and his New Model Army of some twelve thousand troops, Protestant forces violently crushed the Catholic resistance and by 1652 had restored order.[17]

Vicious sectarian warfare, accompanied by famine and plague, stifled Ireland's growth and discouraged the migration of Scots Protestants to Ulster between 1640 and 1660. Scottish immigration resumed, however, after 1674, thanks to the reinvigorated plantation efforts inspired by the confiscation and redistribution of Catholic lands after the 1641 Rising, and continued with only one major interruption until 1715. That interruption, another war between Catholics and Protestants in Ireland, was provoked by the English Parliament's "Glorious Revolution" (1688–1689) against their Stuart monarch, King James II (also James VII of Scotland), son of Charles I, and a Catholic who inherited the throne upon the death of his brother, Charles II, in 1685. When James II's wife gave birth to a male heir whom the English nobility feared would be raised as a Catholic, a group of English noblemen invited James's Dutch Protestant son-in-law and nephew, William of Orange, and his Protestant wife, Mary (James II's daughter) to assume the English throne. Initially, this "Glorious Revolution" in government was notable for its peacefulness. When William arrived from the Netherlands with an invasion force, James II fled to France, paving the way for William and Mary to be crowned joint rulers in 1689. Peace did not last for long, however, because some in England, and many in Scotland and Ireland, did not accept these new monarchs as legitimate. These Jacobites (supporters of James), as they called themselves, were mostly Catholics; their goal was to promote their own interests by restoring the Catholic James to the throne. Thus, when the exiled James, accompanied by a large number of French troops, landed in Ireland in 1689 to fight for the throne through the backdoor of Ireland, he ignited a war with Protestant forces under William. Nearly eighteen months later, in 1690, William's decisive victory at the Battle of the Boyne, north of Dublin, crushed James's efforts, and James fled back to France in defeat.

William's triumph, which was sealed with the Treaty of Limerick in 1691, was immensely important for Ireland's Protestants, for it secured their ascendency and ensured the continuance of the Ulster Plantation; it also brought more confiscated land into circulation.[18] For Lowland Scots who were at the same time facing famine caused by harvest failures in Scotland, William's victory, the return of peace, and bumper harvests that created grain surpluses in Ulster inspired a new surge of emigration. During the 1690s, approximately fifty thousand Scots men, women, and children left their homeland and immigrated to Ulster. Many of them hailed from the southwest of Scotland, a region whose staunch Presbyterian inhabitants had strongly resisted Stuart attempts to control the Church of Scotland. These new arrivals put the final seal on a Scots Protestant community in Ulster and ensured its longevity. Estimates are approximate, but a total of sixty thousand to one hundred thousand Scots relocated to Ulster between 1650 and 1700. This meant that Ulster probably had about two hundred thousand Scots Protestant residents by 1715, who accounted for one-third of the province's total population of six hundred thousand.[19] Thus, in a century's time, and despite the setbacks caused by two especially violent sectarian wars, Scots newcomers had established themselves as a substantial Protestant minority in Ulster. Eastern Ulster, according to one historian, was almost "an extension of West Scotland," while western Ulster had lost much of its Catholic character.[20]

As with any migrant group, a combination of push and pull factors drove these thousands of Scots to relocate. Most were Lowlanders from the broad Midland Valley, which included Glasgow and the country's wealthiest area in and near Edinburgh, or the rural borderlands with England; some were also from one of the southwestern coastal islands.[21] Although political concerns, particularly shifting clan power dynamics, drove some to leave, most were driven by economic concerns. During the sixteenth century, the population in the Scottish Lowlands had increased rapidly, spurring trade and rising prices. Royal authority in the region had also strengthened, which meant higher church tithes and new land policies that favored consolidation and greater oversight. At the same time, many Scottish landlords (or *lairds*) had reorganized their estates and instituted more rational land tenure policies, which led to rapid and steep rises in rents for tenants and a new emphasis on cash rather than in-kind payments.

For the privileged minority of Lowland landlords and merchants, these changes generated a prosperity that left them eagerly seeking new kinds of investment opportunities that Scotland did not offer. By contrast, for the majority, who consisted of tenant farmers and laborers and their families, Scotland's changed demography and economy had harsh, even dire, consequences. High prices, high rents, and an increasingly cash-based economy squeezed the resources of tenant and laboring families, creating a growing population of landless poor who had few prospects. With so many living on the edge, when harvests failed in the 1690s, famine was the result. Thus, many Lowland Scots, whether privileged or poor, had reasons to want to leave their homeland during the seventeenth century.[22]

Life in Ulster

"Ulster provided boundless opportunities" for emigrant Lowland Scots.[23] Chief among its enticements was the promise of obtaining land that had been confiscated from Irish natives. To attract the best men to serve as the linchpins of Ulster's Protestant plantation, the English offered privileged Scots (and English) gentlemen, and some military and government officials, one-thousand- to two-thousand-acre tracts of confiscated and potentially productive land. The undertakers of these lands were then supposed to work for English colonial interests in Ireland by investing in or "improving" their granted lands; they were to construct a bawn (a defensive, walled enclosure) and a substantial house or castle on their properties, and they were to parcel out their lands to hard-working Protestant tenant and laboring families who would till the soil and pasture livestock. The undertakers' investments, aided by a variety of tax incentives, would in turn inspire the development of processing sites and markets and towns and spur the growth of internal commerce and communication networks. The goal was to make Ulster "an early modern enterprise zone."[24]

Although the Ulster plantation involved far more adaptation to local circumstances than the English expected, the expansion of Ulster's population and commercial economy during the second half of the seventeenth century attests that the undertakers took their charge seriously and that tenants responded in kind. The Scots gentry, in particular, did much to foster the immigration of other Scots; they brought in laborers and skilled artisans to complete construction projects and encouraged Scots tenant families to immigrate by offering them inexpensive and long lease terms of twenty-one to thirty-one years or "three lives," which was typically interpreted as the lives of the tenant, his son, and his grandson. Such recruitment practices, particularly the enticement of multigenerational access to land on reasonable terms, encouraged the migration of a broad cross-section of Lowland Scots society who emigrated in family groups, rather than as single individuals, and who arrived committed to the long-term establishment of new lives in Ulster.[25]

Scots migrants were also drawn to Ireland's abundant and largely unexploited natural resources, which included coastal fisheries and woodlands for the harvesting of timber. Such abundance, along with the vagaries of an Irish economy that depended on exports for growth, encouraged diverse economic pursuits among settlers as strategies for survival and profit. The first wave of settlers typically grew grain, often barley and oats, while exploiting fish and timber as sources of additional capital.[26]

Beginning in the 1650s, these patterns shifted, as the new, larger influx of settler families felt the economic pinch of contracting resources and experienced the opportunities and constraints posed by new economic regulations that aimed to subordinate Ireland's economy to England's. Tillage of grain remained a mainstay across Ulster, and in the West, many Scots settlers and their families continued, like Alexander Crawford, to earn part of their living from the sea. But with the fisheries and timber in decline, especially in eastern Ulster, the descendants of the first settlers and newcomers arriving after 1650 more often adopted mixed farming, adding livestock, primarily sheep and cattle, and the associated manufacture of woolen and linen yarn and cloth, to supplement their incomes. For those willing to diversify, Ireland's dependent status in a more tightly regulated English economic system sometimes worked to their favor because of the exclusive market access it offered for select Irish exports. Although the English prohibited the export of finished Irish woolens in 1698 because of competition with their own finished goods, raw wool, wool yarn, and hide exports from Ireland continued, helping to fuel England's growing textile industries; Ireland's salted-beef exports, meanwhile, fed English colonists in North America and the Caribbean, and Europeans on the Continent.[27]

The transformative potential of economic diversification was most evident in Ulster's linen industry, which took off during the eighteenth century. Linen weaving was not new to Ulster; early Scots settlers, who were already familiar with growing flax, spinning yarn, and weaving linen in Scotland, had produced some linen, mostly yarn, once they arrived in Ireland, but only on a small scale and mostly for local consumption. By 1700, however, because of war with France, which increased English demand for products such as linen sailcloth and sacking, and a 1696 English law that encouraged Irish linen production by allowing duty-free exports to England and Scotland, this cottage industry had begun to grow into a larger-scale, more organized manufacture and trade, especially in eastern Ulster. When another trade law in 1705 exempted Irish linens from the Navigation Acts, thereby opening colonial

In this illustration, an Irish farmer in Ulster's County Down plows his land while another sows the flaxseed that will eventually be made into linen cloth, as the farmer's wife, seated with their children, summons him to break for lunch. This is one of twelve prints created by William Hincks in 1783 that depict the Irish linen industry. (William Hincks. *To His Excellency the Lord Lieutenant General and General Governor of Ireland . . . This View taken near Scaroa in the County of Downe, representing ploughing, sowing the flax seed and harrowing; is dedicated by . . . Wm. Hincks.* Engraving. Library of Congress, Prints and Photographs Division, Washington, D.C.)

American markets to direct shipments from Ireland, the trade's economic significance in Ulster was sealed. Production expanded quickly, as did exports of linen yarn and cloth, which went mostly to British ports. By the 1720s, linen cloth made up nearly a quarter of Ireland's total value of exports and rose to two-thirds of the value by 1788. Just as significant, Ireland's growing linen trade helped to realize key goals of the Ulster plantation by stimulating the founding of new towns, fairs, and markets, by inspiring the construction of a communications infrastructure of roads, by creating a vast new demand for specialized artisans and merchants to support the trade, and by bringing much-needed specie into cash-poor Ireland.[28]

Ulster's Scots settlers played pivotal roles in all aspects of this trade. When production began to accelerate in a decentralized fashion in the countryside during the final decades of the seventeenth century, it did so initially through mostly top-down pressure exercised by Protestant landlords who began cultivating flax, encouraging their tenants' wives to spin it into linen yarn, and then establishing new markets for its sale. By the 1720s, and especially by the 1730s to 1750s, when the trade expanded most dramatically, there was also considerable bottom-up involvement from Ulster's tenant farm families, who found they could mortgage their leases for the capital to begin their own, independent production. The Irish Linen Board, founded in 1711, aided their participation in various paternalistic and philanthropic ways; the gentry trustees of the board subsidized the cost of flaxseed and spinning and weaving equipment and oversaw the industry by regulating the kind of cloth produced, teaching proper techniques of production, and encouraging apprenticeships for weavers.

Consequently, linen manufacture became a vital household-based enterprise in Ulster, which built on the division of labor between husbands and wives and may have reinforced the status distinctions between them. Still, the economic rewards for participating in this industry were high, especially in eastern Ulster. Farm families found they could make considerable profit by converting their grain lands to flax. Although men and boys controlled these agricultural tasks, once the flax was harvested, women and girls processed and spun the flax into yarn. Some girls even attended spinning schools run by the wives of Linen Board trustees. In Ireland, unlike in other places in Europe, spinning remained exclusively women's work. But once the flax was spun into yarn or thread, men again dominated and controlled the weaving and bleaching of linen. Men also undertook other aspects of the trade. Linen production, for example, created new demands for retailers and haulers to oversee the emerging trade and distribution networks; and fairs, overseen by linen merchants, who were also men, arose for buying and selling linen domestically.[29]

Also important was the Atlantic World dimension of the linen trade. American colonial demand for Irish linen, particularly the inexpensive plain white and brown varieties used to clothe slaves and servants, coupled with a growing Irish demand for the American-produced flaxseed needed to produce it, set the stage for a reciprocal and profitable international commerce linking Ireland with America, which came to incorporate the trans-Atlantic immigrant and servant trades too. As one historian notes, before 1760, "roughly 70 percent" of the more inexpensive varieties of Irish linen were sent to markets in North America; and in just the three years between 1768 and 1771, "about 4.4 million yards of Irish linen, or about 21 percent of Ireland's total export, was sent across the Atlantic."[30] Thus, Ireland developed close commercial ties to Britain's North American colonies during the eighteenth century. As a result, Irish port cities grew quickly as urban merchants and shippers scrambled

In this illustration by William Hincks depicting the Irish linen industry, four Irish women, accompanied by a young boy and several pets, work inside an Ulster dwelling house to spin, reel, and boil the flax into linen thread. This scene is a strong reminder that linen production, first in Ulster and later in Pennsylvania, was a family enterprise in which women, and even children, played crucial roles. (William Hincks. *To the right hon'able the Earl of Moira, this plate, taken on the spot in the County of Downe, representing spinning, reeling with the clock reel, and boiling the yarn; is most respectfully dedicated by . . . Wm. Hincks.* London: Publish'd as the Act directs, by R. Pollard, Spafields, 1791 June 20. Engraving. Library of Congress, Prints and Photographs Division, Washington, D.C.)

to define their places in this lucrative international commerce. Belfast and its merchant community, in particular, saw some of the greatest benefits from the Atlantic linen and flaxseed trades. By 1730, the city had grown to be Ireland's third largest port, behind Dublin and Cork. Londonderry (Derry) was close behind. By the eighteenth century, it was the second largest port in the North.[31]

The participation of Ulster's Scots in the linen trade transformed their community by encouraging the kind of entrepreneurial activity and embrace of the market economy that many setters had sought but could not find in their Scottish homelands. Men of all ranks saw economic gains from their work as farmers, weavers, bleachers, and retailers, while women, through their work as spinners, gained some economic clout in the household and the marketplace. The trade also fostered the growth of a specialized and commercialized occupational and class structure. Ulster Scots society had always included a wealthy rural gentry and a large mass of tenants and laborers, many of whom were impoverished. By the eighteenth century, because of the linen trade, it also included a rising class of wealthy merchants and professionals and a sizable middling rank of better-off tenants, retailers, and artisans. What is more, increased income from the linen trade helped to redefine social relations within the settler community. With more cash in their pockets, merchants, tenants, artisans, and their families were able to challenge the cultural and political hegemony of Ulster's Protestant landed gentry, setting precedents that would carry over into Pennsylvania.[32]

Despite geographic and economic diversity and even some class competition among Ulster's Scots settlers in the eighteenth century, their religion held them together. Most were "stout Presbyterians who valued education and embraced a church that emphasized discipline and conformity."[33] Like all Scots Presbyterians, these settlers were adherents of the Calvinism John Knox had brought to Scotland from Geneva in 1560. The church Knox and his followers then devised was structured around congregations led by highly educated ministers and elders chosen from the worthiest congregants; Scots Presbyterianism was therefore simultaneously hierarchical and highly localized. It was also intensely communal. In contrast to their fellow Calvinists, the Puritans, who emphasized salvation of the individual, Presbyterians held that salvation would be achieved collectively. This belief encouraged congregations to work together, always under the leadership of their minister, to achieve spiritual grace through Bible reading, catechism, and psalm singing or by listening to sermons.[34] Presbyterian worship was highly structured and community based; ministers were important spiritual and social leaders, while congregations were the foundation of moral guidance and civil discipline within their communities.[35]

Scots migrants to Ulster brought their Presbyterianism with them from Scotland. Over the course of the seventeenth century, and particularly after 1650, they worked to define a congregational system like the one they had known in Scotland by erecting meetinghouses, installing ministers, and founding regional governing bodies of ministers and church elders called presbyteries to guide spiritual and civil affairs. By the eighteenth century, they were the largest Protestant group in Ulster. Nonetheless, as one historian explains, they "remained on the middle rung of a tripartite hierarchy of status and privilege: Anglican, Presbyterian, and Catholic." This position fostered frustration and sometimes resulted in a siege-like mentality.[36] As dissenters in Ireland who did not conform to the state-sponsored Church of Ireland, Scots Presbyterians found themselves in a cooperative but tense relationship with

Ireland's English (mostly Anglican) settlers as the two groups struggled collectively to maintain power while containing large numbers of Irish Catholics who resented, and even hated, them as colonizers. These challenges encouraged the Scots Presbyterians to delineate their religious community in ways that were unlike what they had done in Scotland. Because so much was at stake, Ulster Presbyterianism took on a tightly knit, all-embracing quality. With congregations as their focal point, Ulster Scots ministers and laity from all economic and social levels joined together in their shared spiritual experiences and the quiet performance of their moral duties. Their "comprehensive system of religious and moral discipline" was harsh.[37] The church (*kirk*) session, consisting of its minister and lay elders, regulated and united individual congregations through scrutiny of members' moral behavior and the threat of ostracism. Still, with ministers chosen by their congregations, Ulster Presbyterian congregations also had strong democratic elements.[38]

That these Scots settlers established over a hundred congregations and nine presbyteries by 1700 attests to their success in defining their community. The founding of the General Synod of Ulster in 1690 was their crowning achievement. With the establishment of this synod, Ulster Presbyterians had their own national, ecclesiastical court, wholly separate from the Church of Scotland, to oversee church affairs in the province. Its existence confirmed the church's real and symbolic role as a primary source of group identity in Ulster and proved that these Scots Presbyterians were there to stay.[39]

Shifting Circumstances in the Eighteenth Century

By 1700, after a century of immigration, with some Scots settlers firmly established and others still arriving, Ulster had become a critical meeting ground for Scots, English, and native Irish. Its society has been described as "a complex series of overlapping layers."[40] But as the eighteenth century progressed, those layers and the conditions that had created them grew increasingly unstable, and Ulster became a less hospitable place for its Scots inhabitants. New, more exclusionary British policies provoked a distrust of the English, while increased economic competition, agricultural downturn, and recession undermined Scots' access to opportunity in Ulster. Frustrated by their circumstances, many of Ulster's Scots settlers, including recent arrivals and those whose families had been there for several generations, set out across the Atlantic to Pennsylvania and other destinations in British North America.

Scots settlers had many reasons for leaving eighteenth-century Ulster. A rising tide of religious persecution was among the most important. Ulster Presbyterians had always occupied an ambiguous position in Ireland. Although the English had recruited them to colonize Ulster, the Presbyterian Church to which most belonged did not have the official standing in Ireland that it had in Scotland. Rather, because of Ireland's dependent relationship to England, the Church of Ireland, which was part of the Anglican Communion, held that privileged status. During the seventeenth century, a time of intense religious turmoil and political revolution in England, Scotland, and Ireland, the English had tolerated the Scots Presbyterians in Ireland, encouraging them to join with other Protestants to help subdue and contain the often rebellious Roman Catholic Irish natives.[41]

By the eighteenth century, however, English-imposed Penal Laws, which denied full citizenship to Irish Catholics, began to affect Presbyterians. Most notable was the Test Act of 1704, which required Presbyterians, much like Catholics, to pay tithes to the Church of Ireland. It also subjected their marriages to review by Anglican ecclesiastical courts, prohibited them from maintaining their own schools, and restricted their access to civil and military office holding. Although this act was not enforced consistently against the Scots, it nonetheless had consequences. Furthermore, as Great Britain (newly created by the 1707 Act of Union, which united England and Scotland) worked to define its identity as a nation, it intensified its efforts to assert the preeminence of Anglicanism in Ireland, and being a dissenter in Ulster began to carry a stigma, which was accompanied by economic and political penalties. Some Ulster Presbyterian gentry chose to conform to the Church of Ireland to gain access to offices of influence. For the mass of Ulster Scots, however, the Test Act generated a climate of hostility toward the English and Presbyterian gentry who conformed. Scots Presbyterians took intense pride in their staunch Protestantism; their beliefs, they held, should guarantee them all the rights and privileges of British citizenship while clearly distinguishing them from Catholics. To be officially stigmatized as dissenters and even disenfranchised by the Test Act was deeply frustrating.[42]

Religious grievances undoubtedly influenced the decision to emigrate. Yet contrary to long-standing assumptions and much popular lore, religious motives were not the primary factor pushing the Ulster Scots out of Ireland and to America; economic conditions were far more significant. As the letters by Alexander Crawford and Henry Johnston illustrate, by the eighteenth century, economic misery had come to mark the lives of many Ulster Protestants. Ireland was no longer the place where the mass of Scots settlers could find opportunity.

Many of the economic hardships in eighteenth-century Ulster stemmed from the same economic developments that had attracted so many Scots to Ireland in the first place. Ulster's late seventeenth-century economic growth and diversification had fostered occupational diversity and class disparity among its Scots settler population. From the start, however, the opportunities for landownership under English rule had disproportionately benefited the more economically privileged Scots who had been able to assume ownership of confiscated estates. The mass of Ulster's Scots settlers saw fewer benefits; they were poor to middling tenant farmers who worked others' lands under a system that mostly functioned smoothly as long as the terms of their leases were generous. By the 1710s, increased competition for land—triggered by economic improvements, including the development of the linen industry and the arrival of a large number of new Scottish immigrants to Ulster during the 1690s—tipped the economic balance in favor of landlords, who, like Alexander Murray, were often absentees. With lands in demand and leases expiring, landlords raised rents and offered more restrictive lease terms in a trend that continued for the next century. Then, a series of poor harvests between 1716 and 1723, between 1727 and 1728, and again during the 1730s led to economic depression, food shortages, and even outright famines in 1727 and 1740. For the mass of Ulster's agrarian Protestants who were long-term tenants like Alexander Crawford and his family, rent increases, especially when combined with economic downturn, brought severe economic distress of the kind that bred resentment, especially against absentee landlords, and inspired some to leave.[43]

Instability in the linen industry in the eighteenth century also created economic problems. Linen production, as we have seen, was an important supplement to farming for many families in Ulster; for some, it was a basic strategy for survival. But because the price of linen cloth increased little and few changes were made to improve the efficiency of production, the supplemental income farm families derived from linen production did not keep pace with their rising rents. The industry also weathered its own recession between 1718 and 1729 and a period of general stagnation and decline after 1770. The effects of these downturns in one of Ulster's major industries rippled across country and town, causing what Henry Johnston describes to his brother as "woe & misery" for tens of thousands of rural producers, processors, and weavers, as well as urban haulers, retailers, and overseas merchants.[44]

Faced with rising rents, stagnant wages, decreased access to land, and declining sources of additional income from the linen trade, as well as religious discrimination, and encouraged by letters from friends and relatives, newspaper stories about the high standard of living and quality of life in North America, and ship agents who were eager to fill their ships' holds with emigrants, many Irish Scots decided to emigrate again, this time making the bigger move across the Atlantic.

2

COMING TO PENNSYLVANIA

We was three days on our journey coming from Harrisses ferry here. . . . [W]e could not make much speed on account of the child[ren]. . . . [T]hey could not get on as fast [as] Jane and me[.] I think we will like this part of the country when we get our cabbin bilt[.] I put it on a level peese [piece] of groun[d] near the road . . . at the fut [foot] of a hill. . . . [T]here is a fine stream of water that comes from a spring a half a mile south of where our cabbin is bilt. (James Magraw, Middle Spring, Cumberland County, Pennsylvania, to John Magraw, Paxton Township, Lancaster County, Pennsylvania, May 21, 1733)[1]

JAMES MAGRAW, his wife, Jane, and their children were among the first Ulster colonists to settle west of the Susquehanna River, near present-day Shippensburg, in the early 1730s. Although details about the Magraw family's emigration from their home in County Fermanagh, Ulster, to Pennsylvania during the 1720s are sparse, evidence suggests that their experience was much like that of other eighteenth-century Ulster Scots Irish who came to North America. The Magraw family left Ireland during one of the peak decades of Ulster immigration to the American colonies. Like the majority of Ulster emigrants, they traveled as an extended family—two brothers and their wives and children—and paid their own passage across the Atlantic. Thus, they arrived in Pennsylvania as free people.

Although many Ulster immigrants settled and remained in or near Philadelphia, a growing colonial metropolis that offered abundant employment opportunities, others, like the Magraws, moved west to the colony's frontiers, drawn by an invitation from the Penn family's chief official in the colony, the Ulster-born Quaker James Logan, to buy cheap land. Logan sought to encourage the founding of new Ulster Scots settlements in the colony's south-central interior (then the colony's western frontier) because he believed that the Ulster Scots' Irish experience as a Protestant minority living among an often hostile Roman Catholic majority had primed them to act as a defensive buffer against possible invasions by Indians or the colony's Maryland rivals. Creating a buffer was vitally important in a colony led by pacifist Quakers who shunned militarization.[2] During the 1720s, many immigrant families, including the Magraws, responded to Logan's invitation and took up lands on the east bank of the Susquehanna near Harris's Ferry (present-day Harrisburg) in what became Donegal and Paxton Townships of Lancaster County, which was founded in 1729. Once there, living among the region's Delaware (Lenni Lenape) peoples, they farmed, traded, founded new Presbyterian congregations, and established townships with Ulster names such as Derry. The formation of the Lancaster-based Donegal Presbytery followed in 1732, confirming their increasing presence in the area.

When colony officials began granting licenses (promissory notes for a future deed) to the region west of the Susquehanna River after 1730, James and Jane Magraw and others moved onto Indian lands. As James's note to his brother suggests, despite the considerable risk in settling an area of the colony that had not yet been purchased from its native claimants, the family found abundant, fertile, well-watered lands in the Cumberland Valley. They worked hard to put down roots there, building new lives from scratch while living among the Indians who remained in the area. For those Scots Irish immigrants who came to Pennsylvania looking for land, the risks taken by colonists like the Magraws were significant. Driven by Logan's encouragement and the lure of affordable lands, although they never intended to become frontier people, these Ulster newcomers spearheaded the European colonial settlement frontier in the mid-Atlantic while claiming the Cumberland Valley as one of the principal cultural hearths of the Scots Irish in America.[3]

This chapter traces the migratory patterns of Scots Irish immigrants like the Magraw family who came to Pennsylvania during the eighteenth century. It identifies the factors that drew them to Pennsylvania and outlines the defining characteristics of their migration, which was one component of a larger, eighteenth-century Irish diaspora. It also describes the diversity of this group and their experiences. These emigrants came from different socioeconomic backgrounds and hailed from different places in Ulster, including border counties just outside Ulster. Once in Pennsylvania, they settled in the East and West, living urban and rural lives. James and Jane Magraw's story thus represents one of the many experiences of Ulster immigrants in Pennsylvania.

Why Pennsylvania?

When Ulster had lost its appeal to the Scots Irish and they began to look to Britain's American colonies for relief, the colony they turned to most often was Pennsylvania. Its two principal ports of New Castle (now in Delaware) and Philadelphia became their major migration destinations during the eighteenth century.

The founder and proprietor of the colony of Pennsylvania, William Penn (1644–1718), was a devoted Quaker (having converted to its tenets in 1667), a member of a privileged English gentry family, and an eager entrepreneur; his personal history thus foreshadowed a colony that would be a mix of religious idealism, commerce, and economic speculation. As one of West New Jersey's Quaker proprietors during the 1670s, Penn brought some experience in colony building to planning his colony. When in 1680 King Charles II granted him the lands that would become Pennsylvania in return for a debt owed to his father, Penn set out to create his own "holy experiment." To do so, he grounded his colony's governance in Quaker principles. These included liberty of conscience (the right to believe in the faith you wish) and religious toleration (the right to worship as you wish, as long as you were Christian and preferably not Roman Catholic). Because he had suffered harassment and even imprisonment in England for his Quaker beliefs, Penn held that religious persecution was "illegal, immoral, and contrary to both reason and nature," and he said it would not be tolerated in his colony.[4] Just as important, as a corollary stemming from his observation that civil disorders more often "arose out of a 'Narrowness of Spirit,'" Penn embraced the radical view that religious and cultural pluralism would be the building blocks of his colony.[5] Pennsylvania was to be a place where all colonists (whether they were English or not, Quakers or non-Quakers) would enjoy liberty of conscience, religious toleration, separation of church and state, and the other rights and privileges English subjects took pride in possessing.

Penn also lay the groundwork for an economically successful colony. Because many Quakers had come to accept prosperity as being compatible with their spiritual beliefs, Penn's "holy experiment" had pragmatic and even self-interested economic dimensions; Penn, the businessman and speculator, intended to profit from his colony. To accomplish his goal, he had to attract investors and colonists to fund, settle, and build his colony for him, and that meant careful planning and recruitment. Penn began by purchasing Delaware Valley lands from the Delawares. He commissioned the Irish Quaker Thomas Holme to survey the site for the colony's principal city, Philadelphia. Holme chose a central-square, grid-plan design that was similar to the ones the English employed in Ulster towns like Londonderry (Derry); such towns had been planned to model Protestant commercial life for the native Irish. With access to land secured and plans for a commercial port city in hand, Penn enticed wealthy investors to his colonial project and used their money as seed capital to launch his colony in 1682.[6]

To recruit settlers to populate the colony's three counties with farms and build the houses, wharves, and businesses that would be needed to make Philadelphia's grid productive, Penn wrote promotional tracts. In them, he described Pennsylvania's abundant natural resources, particularly the lands he had available for purchase; he also outlined the colony's considerable prospects for growth and development and offered potential settlers directions about how to obtain passage across the Atlantic. He distributed these works in England and Ireland; Dutch- and German-language versions went to the European continent. Finally, to put his plans in motion, he appointed agents in various port cities, including Dublin, to aid potential colonists in booking their voyages, obtaining indentures, and purchasing lands.[7]

Penn's promotional strategy worked; immigrants flocked to the colony from England, Scotland, Ireland, and the European continent, and Pennsylvania grew quickly as a result. As the eighteenth century dawned, the colony had attracted nearly eighteen thousand European colonists to its borders in less than twenty years.[8] With wheat and other grain crops emerging as the mainstays of the colony's agricultural economy, Pennsylvania was on its way to becoming a breadbasket for the Atlantic, and Philadelphia, the center of this commerce, was rapidly emerging as a major colonial port. Penn had "organized the fastest and most efficient colonization in the seventeenth-century English empire," even though he never profited sufficiently from the colony to offset his considerable debts.[9] For European colonists in the eighteenth century, however, Pennsylvania had much to recommend it. The colony had a reputation for peaceful relations with the local Indians, for its acceptance of cultural pluralism, and for its many natural, agricultural, and commercial resources.

Pennsylvania had particular appeal to the Ulster Scots Irish. In contrast to Ireland, or the New England colonies, Pennsylvania's inclusive governing principles and structures promised Scots Irish Presbyterians that they would be part of a civil society where they would no longer bear the stigma of being religious dissenters. Pennsylvania's expanding economy was also dynamic enough to accommodate the varied pursuits of Ulster settlers who were accustomed to balancing farming with manufacturing and trade. As the fastest growing city in the colonies, and the largest on the eve of the American Revolution, Philadelphia, which had expanded from a few hundred settlers in the early 1690s to approximately forty thousand inhabitants by 1776, offered newcomers the chance to participate in an urban commercial economy linked to Atlantic World markets.[10] Unlike the older and more densely settled New England colonies where obtaining property was difficult, the young colony of Pennsylvania possessed abundant land and a seemingly limitless frontier, if those lands could be obtained peacefully from the Indians.

Among the Ulster Protestant settlers who found Pennsylvania attractive were merchants, most of them Presbyterians, who emigrated from towns such as Belfast with the expectation of building businesses on or near Philadelphia's wharves. Later they might acquire substantial landed estates outside the city. The high demand for skilled and unskilled laborers in the colony also meant that Ulster's poorer sorts could find opportunity too. Although many of them would have to temporarily sacrifice their freedom to immigrate as indentured servants or redemptioners (servants who sailed without a contract and redeemed their costs of passage by selling their labor upon arrival),[11] they could expect to find work once they had completed their terms of service. Ulster's middling sort, however, the tenant farmers and artisans and small-scale traders, especially those involved in linen trade, had the most to gain by coming to Pennsylvania. With reasonably priced, unimproved lots and lands still available, Philadelphia, its Delaware Valley hinterlands, and especially the colony's expanding settlement frontier offered these Protestants the chance to become landowners for the first time in their lives. Because of all that the colony offered, Pennsylvania was widely regarded as British North America's "best poor man's country."[12]

Patterns of Migration

Scots Irish emigration from Ulster to America was a phenomenon of the long eighteenth century; it began slowly in the late seventeenth century and continued until the end of the Napoleonic Wars in 1815. During just over a century's time, somewhere between 250,000 and 500,000 men and women left Ireland for North America, nearly two-thirds of them Scots Irish Presbyterians. They accounted for "30 percent of all European immigrants in that period (and 50 percent between 1776 and 1820)."[13] Moreover, probably 100,000 emigrated directly from Ulster to the colonies just during the years between 1718 and 1775. Patrick Griffin describes this wave of migration as "the single largest movement of any group from the British Isles to British North America during the eighteenth century."[14]

Many of the first emigrants to leave Ireland between 1680 and 1716 sailed to Boston; they were drawn to Massachusetts by the Calvinist beliefs of the colony's Puritan founders. Yet once there, these newcomers found themselves frustrated by the colony's tight land holdings and its established church, which was mostly unwelcoming to them. Their experiences taught others to look elsewhere. During the 1710s, several thousand emigrants also departed for Charles Town, South Carolina, and with bounties to entice them there, others followed. South Carolina remained an important secondary destination for Scots Irish emigrants throughout the century.[15]

Pennsylvania, however, with its religious toleration, abundant economic resources, and an organized Presbytery in Philadelphia by 1706, became the principal migration destination of the Ulster Irish. During the first major uptick in migration during the late 1710s, the colony's Delaware River ports of New Castle (the "Lower Counties" that would later become Delaware) and Philadelphia accounted for more than 50 percent of arrivals from Ulster.[16] According to one estimate, between 1730 and 1775, nearly fifty-two thousand Irish immigrants entered the Delaware Valley.[17] Although Ulster Irish immigration to Pennsylvania occurred steadily throughout the eighteenth century, significant peaks occurred during the late 1710s and 1720s and again during the mid-1760s and early 1770s.

The trigger for the first major wave of emigration during the late 1710s was a rapid rise in lease rates for Ulster lands as the cheap leases of the 1690s expired. Drought and crop failures between 1715 and 1720 compounded the problem of more costly rents, as did a downturn in Irish linen exports to Great Britain. Between 1717 and 1719 some 4,000 to 7,000 people left Ulster ports for America; the majority headed for the Delaware Valley.[18] Of even greater influence was the famine that struck Ireland in 1729; this calamity inspired a short-lived but intense wave of emigration between 1729 and the early 1730s, during which some 15,000 additional Scots Irish departed from Ulster. This first, mass exodus of Irish Protestants inspired some degree of panic in Ireland, where officials feared the departure of so many so quickly might jeopardize Anglo-Protestant control.[19] Pennsylvanians also took note of the arrival of so many Irish newcomers. In 1729 and 1730, for example, nearly 6,000 Irish men and women disembarked in the Delaware Valley—most of them in New Castle—in a surge that was ten times the typical rate of 640 immigrants a year.[20] The provincial secretary, James Logan, began to regret the encouragement he had offered. Expressing the sentiment of others in the colony, Logan fretted that "if Ireland is to send all her inhabitants hither . . . they will make themselves proprietors of the province."[21]

His concerns were not unfounded. There were more Ulster immigrants to come during the 1760s and 1770s in a second, even larger, and more diverse surge of migration that followed the conclusion of the Seven Years' War (or French and Indian War) and preceded the American Revolution. Two peaks also marked this second wave, the first occurring during the mid-1760s, and the second during the early 1770s. Almost three thousand Irish immigrants arrived in the Delaware Valley ports in 1766, while during the largest spike between 1770 and 1775, nearly thirty thousand arrived.[22] As during the earlier surge, economic hardship was the primary motive for leaving Ireland. Ulster residents had again endured bad harvests and rising food costs. Rents for farmlands reached a high point during the 1760s, resulting in the eviction of many Ulster tenants. In County Antrim, in northeastern Ulster, a heightened sense of economic injustice sparked a series of armed protests against rising rents and church tithes by Presbyterian farmers calling themselves the "Hearts of Steel" or "Steelboys."[23] Yet the determining factor in this migratory surge was a crisis in the linen industry, which entered a major depression during the early 1770s. Foreign demand for Irish linen had declined by 50 percent during 1771–1772, sending prices and wages into sharp decline.[24] In response, large numbers of Scots Protestants, many of them town dwellers with strong connections to linen industry, fled Ulster for the Delaware Valley.

Philadelphia played a central role in this second, post-1763 migration. Whereas during the 1710s and 1720s, most Ulster immigrants disembarked at New Castle, by the 1760s, Philadelphia was the primary port-of-entry.[25] This shift made sense. By 1760, Philadelphia had overtaken Boston to become the largest city in the American colonies.[26] It was a vibrant colonial port, where immigrants could find opportunity. Furthermore, Philadelphia's merchants, a sizable number of whom were Irish immigrants themselves by mid-century, maintained extensive trade relationships, and even partnerships, with merchants in Ireland.[27] Irish linen was in high demand in Pennsylvania. Ireland was also significant export market for Pennsylvania's grain, barrel staves, and the flaxseed Ulster's linen weavers needed to grow flax. Flaxseed was the number one export from the Middle Colonies to Ireland by 1770, and it was the third most important export crop Pennsylvania produced.[28] Sustaining the lucrative flaxseed trade generated a huge seasonal demand for shipping between Philadelphia and northern Irish ports such as Belfast and Londonderry (Derry). Most ships departed the Delaware Valley

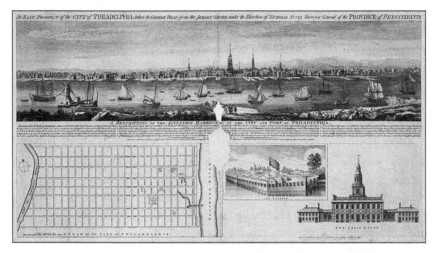

The grid-planned Philadelphia where many Scots Irish immigrants disembarked in 1768 was a thriving port city and expanding political, commercial, and cultural center. (*An East Prospect of the City of Philadelphia; taken by George Heap from the Jersey Shore, under the Direction of Nicholas Scull[,] Surveyor General of the Province of Pennsylvania / Engrav'd by T. Jefferys.* [London]: Publish'd according to Act of Parliament by T. Jefferys near Charing Cross, [1768]. Library of Congress, Prints and Photographs Division, Washington, D.C.)

in December, carrying flaxseed and other agricultural products to Ireland; they returned from Ulster to Philadelphia in the spring, summer, and early fall, their hulls filled with Irish dry goods and their decks with immigrants. By mid-century, Philadelphia's immigrant trade with Ulster was ongoing and highly regularized. It arose to complement an Atlantic trade driven by Ireland's increasing demand for flaxseed and Pennsylvanians' desire for linen, as well as the expanding colony's need for colonists.[29]

With so many ships sailing to the Delaware Valley, migration between Ulster became routine.[30] This situation worked to the advantage of the emigrants. Because ship captains transporting flax and linen could make sufficient profit from their cargoes, they did not have to fill their vessels with indentured servants, which meant that Ulster emigrants had a choice of vessels on which to sail. The trade was competitive enough that shippers actually had to recruit passengers by advertising the comfort and potential security of their vessels. Competition also helped to keep passenger fares relatively low; most emigrants paid about four pounds sterling per person to cross the Atlantic at a time when fifteen to twenty pounds a year constituted a low annual wage in England.[31] What is more, with ships departing from several Ulster ports, emigrants generally did not have to travel far to access overseas transportation, which helped to further trim the total cost of migration. Because of the frequency and regularity of this Atlantic trade, sailing times between Ulster and Pennsylvania, which were never especially long by the standards of the day, gradually decreased. In the 1720s, the trip from Ulster to Philadelphia took between eight and ten weeks; by the 1770s, it generally took seven weeks. Crowding was also relatively minimal and was associated mostly with the heaviest years of migration. Most below-decks living during the voyage was cramped but not jam-packed. In sum, although crossing the Atlantic in the age of sail was always uncomfortable, unpredictable, and sometimes dangerous—and there were certainly some notorious stories of disastrous voyages from Ulster—compared with other eighteenth-century European immigrants, such as the Germans, or enslaved Africans, Ulster's Scots Irish immigrants had a relatively easy journey.[32]

Who Came to Pennsylvania?

Scots Irish immigrants to Pennsylvania were mostly free people who came as members of family, kin, or friendship groups. Whereas the colonial servant trade focused on Dublin and drew mostly southern (often Roman Catholic) Irish to the colonies as laborers, the Ulster immigrant trade was notable for the large number of free people who sailed to America, especially during the peak periods of migration of the 1760s and 1770s. Overall, perhaps 20 percent of those who sailed from Ulster were bound laborers, but sometimes the percentage was lower.[33] Among the bound laborers from Ulster was Andrew Robinson, a twenty-year-old sandy-haired man of "middle stature" who arrived in the Delaware Valley by way of the port of Dublin during the summer of 1750. Robinson worked in Chester County until he and another Irish servant ran away.[34] In contrast to the low percentage of bound laborers from Ulster was the high percentage of free people. One scholar found that 90 percent of the Ulster immigrants who arrived in the Delaware Valley between 1771 and 1772 had paid their own passage to America.[35] Such a figure is extraordinary given another scholar's calculations that during the early 1770s nearly 50 percent of all English and Scottish immigrants arrived in America as either servants or redemptioners.[36]

Most immigrants from southern Ireland, or England and Scotland, were young, unmarried men traveling alone. The pattern of Scots Irish from Ulster, however, was similar to that of German immigrants to the Delaware Valley, who tended to arrive in family groups, especially before 1750.[37] During the post-1763 period, for example, nearly 40 percent of Scots Irish who disembarked at a Delaware Valley port had sailed to America as part of a family or kin group. Those who immigrated as young, unmarried men typically did so as part of a chain of family members who came over one at a time, often as a cost-saving measure, or they came to join friends from Ulster who were already in Pennsylvania. "In the migration flow from Ireland," one historian observes, "the ties of kinship and community, as well as the bonds that linked co-religionists, were important dynamics in driving the transatlantic relocation."[38]

These migratory patterns of the Scots Irish as an ethnic group both confirm and challenge popular portrayals of who came to Pennsylvania and what they did once they got here. The Scots Irish were as well known for being clannish as they were for being rugged individualists. Yet they did not begin their new lives in Pennsylvania alone or in isolation but typically traveled with others and remained deeply embedded in kin, communal, economic, and Presbyterian networks stretching back to Ulster. Once there, as David Noel Doyle observes, "almost all" sought to "reestablish the Ulster priorities of family, kin, and community in more secure circumstance, not to cut loose as frontier individualists."[39]

Just as significant, the number of Scots Irish who paid their way to Pennsylvania reminds us of how many of the men and women who came to the colony—even during the toughest economic times in Ulster—came voluntarily and possessed sufficient economic means to pay their own way across the Atlantic, a major accomplishment during the colonial period. This meant that once they arrived in Pennsylvania, most of them possessed sufficient resources—including economic and communal support networks—to establish themselves, even if that meant taking the risk of migrating into the colony's interior, where they could purchase the least expensive lands cheaply or eke out an existence as squatters. Few left Ireland or arrived in Pennsylvania desperately poor.

James Magraw, who settled with his family in the Cumberland Valley in the 1730s, comes closest to exemplifying the popular prototype of the colonial Scots Irish immigrant as hardy and fearless frontiersman. Magraw, his wife, Jane, and their children emigrated from the area near Maguire's Bridge, a market town in County Fermanagh in southwestern Ulster. Although we know little about their lives there, we can presume that Magraw and his family were farmers, and because they paid for their passage to Pennsylvania, we can surmise that they had some economic resources. We also know that they immigrated as part of an extended family group, which suggests that their move was planned and, because of the timing of their migration during one of the peak periods, that their relocation was probably a response to the economic hardships and decreasing opportunities of the late 1720s. Once in the colony, the Magraws, like many other Scots Irish arrivals of the time, moved west into the colony's interior in search of land. In doing so, they followed James Logan's encouragement to his "brave fellow countrymen" to pioneer the colony's backcountry "as a leading example to others" and to act as a protective buffer. The Magraws found land first on the eastern side of the Susquehanna, in Paxton Township, where they joined at least a hundred other Ulster families who had settled there by 1730. Then they moved again, into the Cumberland Valley, where they helped to pioneer the new settlement of Middle Spring on heavily forested lands still inhabited by Delawares and Shawnees and not yet formally purchased by the colony.[40]

Magraw describes the trepidation he felt about moving into Indian territory, writing that he "fear[ed]" that the many Indians nearby "intend to give us a good deal of trouble and may do us a grate [great] deal of harm."[41] Still, during the so-called long peace that marked Pennsylvania's first half century or so, he and his wife spent most of their days working to locate lands, build a cabin, and plant their first crops of corn and potatoes. In their activities on the frontier, the Magraws became one of the Scots Irish families to pioneer the Cumberland Valley as their "headquarters . . . in Pennsylvania but in America as well."[42] However difficult their frontier lives were, as free people and a family who could afford to purchase land, they had advantages that many other immigrants to the colony did not.

While the Magraws exemplify the experiences of many Ulster emigrants, among the new arrivals to Pennsylvania were more economically privileged families who were Protestant but not Presbyterian. Some hailed from border counties just outside of Ulster. Acknowledging their profiles widens our sense of who these Irish Protestant immigrants were and what their goals were in coming to Pennsylvania. William West Sr., for example, who was born in 1724 in County Sligo, just west of Ulster, in Connaught Province, immigrated to Philadelphia by 1750 with at least one sibling, his brother Francis, and they came as free men, arriving during the thirty-year lull between migration peaks. Once in Philadelphia, West had the means and connections to establish himself as a dry-goods merchant with strong trade ties to Ireland; he also participated in the immigrant and servant trade with his former homeport of Sligo. He was an avid real estate speculator who purchased lots in the new town of Carlisle, a village designed by the proprietor Thomas Penn (William's son) in 1751 and pioneered by West's brother Francis, and in rural Tyrone township, Cumberland County, which was named for a county in Ulster. From the time of his arrival, West played an active role in the colony's

Historic Hope Lodge, in Whitemarsh, was the home of William and Mary West from 1770 to 1782. (Arabsalam. *Hope Lodge*. Photo. 31 August 2006. Wikimedia Commons, https://commons.wikimedia.org/wiki/File:HopeLodge_HistoricSite.JPG.)

fur and skin trades with native peoples and "took a leading role in representing Pennsylvania's interest" in the Ohio Valley during the years leading up to the Seven Years' War by conducting diplomacy, mapping territory, and gathering intelligence.[43] He married Mary Hodge, the daughter of another prosperous merchant in 1757; they had twelve children together.

By all accounts, William West did well for himself in America. His Philadelphia-based business, which was firmly rooted in kin- and Irish-based Protestant networks, some of them Scots, others Anglo, helped to make him a wealthy man by the 1770s. In 1770, he purchased a high-style Georgian estate at Whitemarsh, later named Hope Lodge, just outside the city; he and his wife and family lived there until his death in 1782. He also held various elected and appointed offices, most of which were rooted in Philadelphia. He was a member of the Pennsylvania Assembly during the 1750s, an Indian commissioner in the early 1760s, and later a Revolutionary War patriot. He served as president of the Friendly Sons of St. Patrick and as a member of the Hibernia Fire Company.[44]

Although West had many frontier connections, he chose to live in Philadelphia, where, thanks in part to the help of his brother in Carlisle and various merchant connections in Ireland, he oversaw a thriving Atlantic World commercial network of trade in furs, skins, dry goods, and immigrants that stretched from the Ohio country through Carlisle to Philadelphia and then to Ireland. He took pride in his Irish heritage but had no apparent religious affiliation. West was most certainly Protestant, probably Anglican, though maybe Presbyterian, but he did not attend church, and his business connections included both Presbyterians and Quakers. As a cosmopolitan, successful, powerful, but not especially pious, man of the Atlantic World, West defies popular stereotypes of the Scots Irish, reminding us how diverse Irish emigrants were.[45]

William Irvine, who rose to the rank of brigadier general in the Continental Army during the American Revolution, adds yet another dimension. Irvine, like James and Jane Magraw, came from County Fermanagh in the western reaches of Ulster; he was born near the town of Enniskillen in 1741. Unlike the Magraws, however, Irvine was from a privileged, even noble family whose deep roots in Ulster dated to the time of James I when an ancestor, Sir Christopher Irvine, was granted lands under the terms of the plantation. Irvine was also educated; he had trained in Dublin to be a physician and served in the British Navy as a surgeon during the Seven Years' War. Although we have little information about his migratory journey, he evidently left Ulster in either 1763 or 1764, during the second and larger eighteenth-century migratory surge. He paid his own passage and seems to have sailed alone. Once in Pennsylvania, he followed the path of William West's brother Francis and moved west to Carlisle. Because Carlisle was the principal town of the Cumberland Valley, it drew Scots Irish immigrants with urban or professional interests to its expanding borders. Irvine's close friend (perhaps a relative) from Enniskillen, John Armstrong, was already an established local official and community leader in Carlisle when Irvine arrived. Irvine's brother Mathew also lived nearby. These kin and communal connections probably aided Irvine's transition to Pennsylvania and helped him establish his practice as a physician in town.

Although Irvine was surrounded by his fellow country men and women in the Cumberland Valley, he seems to have been restless. Into the early 1770s he continued to speak of "his desire to 'go to Sea and afterward settle in Ireland' again." But then his circumstances changed. In 1772, he married Ann Callender, the eldest daughter of the well-known merchant, fur trader, mill owner, land speculator, and militia captain Robert Callender of Carlisle, also

William Irvine was a university-educated former British naval surgeon who emigrated from Enniskillen, Ulster, in the 1760s and made his new American life in the backcountry town of Carlisle. There he married Ann Callender, the eldest daughter of the well-known Scots Irish fur trader Robert Callender. (*William Irvine* [1748–1804]. James Lambdin [copied from an original by Robert Pine]. Philadelphia History Museum Collection, The Historical Society of Pennsylvania Collection. Gift of William A. Irvine, 1865 [HSP.1865.1P]. Courtesy of the Philadelphia History Museum at the Atwater Kent, The Historical Society of Pennsylvania Collection.)

Scots Irish, but an Anglican rather than a Presbyterian. Marriage rooted Irvine in Carlisle, where he and Ann, and eventually their eleven children, made their home. Then the American Revolution began, and Irvine, like many other Scots Irish in Pennsylvania's westernmost county of Cumberland (formed in 1750), joined the American cause early, volunteering for Continental Army service in 1775 and remaining for the duration of the war. He ended his service as the commander of Fort Pitt. For Irvine, the revolution marked a critical turning point. With the war, he put his practice as a physician aside and launched a career of civil, military, and political service that took him and his family to Philadelphia in 1800 and continued until his death at age sixty-three in 1804.[46]

As the life experiences of James Magraw, William West, and William Irvine demonstrate, the Scots Irish who came to Pennsylvania defy easy categorization. They were neither uniformly poor nor uniformly rich; they came from different regions of Ulster, and sometimes from counties just outside the province's borders; their family backgrounds varied, as did their economic and professional interests; and although Protestant, not all were Presbyterians.

Once in America, their lives and those of their families followed different trajectories. Some lived on the frontier and worked as farmers, some lived in the Delaware Valley and made a more lucrative living as merchants, others lived in one of the colony's backcountry towns, working as professionals or in a retail or service occupation. Despite these differences, their migration experiences fit patterns that were characteristic of other eighteenth-century Ulster emigrants. All three men arrived in Pennsylvania as free men, and this status gave them advantages many other colonial immigrants who arrived as bound laborers did not have. They also immigrated as part of a family group or, like Irvine, as one link in a chain of migration of friends and kin. Because they did not come alone but moved within deeply embedded networks of support, they were less likely to fail.

3

BUILDING COMMUNITIES

John M'Cullogh was born may 27—1748—it being friday about one o[']Clock and on the 12th day of the moon[']s age.

the red Sea is 15 mil[e]s broad and 35 fadom [fathoms] deep. . . .[T]he wall of babl [Babel] was 87 fo[o]t wi[d]th . . .

I did hall [haul] in Wheat July the 3 and [s]owed flex [flax] and buck Wheat Jun[e]—28 and I Sowed buck Wheat July—the 11th— 1750 and thrush [threshed] flex [flax] July the—12th.

I did Sow turneps [turnips] July the 4th and Rept [reaped] oats July the 5th. . . . I did Sow turnips July the 23[.]

December the 11[,] 1750 Willem [William] Carson to Work don[e]—24 yeards [yards] of Lincey [linsey] Woven 3 y[ar]ds Strip[p] ed with 2 Shitels [shuttles—used in weaving] and 6 yeards [yards] and a half with 3 Shitels [shuttles] more. (From the journal of James McCullough, near Chambersburg, Pennsylvania, in what is now Franklin County)[1]

JAMES McCULLOUGH was a Scots Irish weaver and farmer who lived with his wife, Martha, and their growing family on the frontier of south-central Pennsylvania during the late 1740s and 1750s. They were newcomers to Pennsylvania, having emigrated together from County Londonderry (Derry) to New Castle in 1745. They remained in New Castle for perhaps five years, where, as McCullough notes, their son, John, was born. Then, in about 1750, James, Martha, their son, and a daughter, along with other Mc-

Cullough kin, moved west into what would become Franklin County (then Cumberland County). They settled in Antrim Township, not far from Chambersburg, in an area pioneered by other Ulster immigrants in the 1730s, as the township's name suggests. Once there, McCullough purchased a two-hundred-acre farm at a sheriff's auction, and he and his family settled into their new life on Pennsylvania's culturally diverse frontier.

Although irregular spelling and usage makes McCullough's journal challenging to read, it offers insights into the daily life of a proto-typical Scots Irish family on the frontiers of colonial Pennsylvania. It reveals that the McCullough family led a busy but mundane existence in the years before the Seven Years' War. Family stood first and foremost, as McCullough's recording of the birth of his first son suggests. Faith rooted in scripture was also vitally important. The McCullough family were Presbyterians, as the quoted references to the Red Sea and the Tower of Babel from the Old Testament confirm. We learn also that McCullough was a skilled weaver and that he and his wife farmed and produced cloth. In Pennsylvania as in Ulster, weaving was a family- and even community-based enterprise. James sowed and harvested the flax with help from family, friends, or laborers; Martha spun the fibers into yarn or thread; James then wove the linen cloth that he could market to his neighbors. Aside from flax, the family farmed grain and grew peas, corn, turnips, and potatoes. McCullough's journal, which also functions as an informal business ledger, records the cloth he wove and sold, the crops the family planted and harvested, and the goods they bought with what they earned.

The activities that James McCullough recorded in his journal remind us of the continued importance of kin, community, and Protestantism, specifically Presbyterianism, to Scots Irish colonists in Pennsylvania, and the fundamental role that family and friends, religion, and exchange played as building blocks of the Scots Irish communities that arose all across Pennsylvania during the eighteenth century.

This chapter focuses on the multiple communities the Scots Irish founded after they arrived in Pennsylvania, detailing some of the varied settings—rural and urban, western and eastern—where Scots Irish colonists settled and the range of economic activities they engaged in to make their way in America. Yet it also addresses the key building blocks of community, including family, friendship, and particularly Presbyterianism, which linked these diverse colonists and their settlements together and generated cohesion among them. Still, when the momentous religious revival the Great Awakening swept through Pennsylvania, it bitterly divided the members of these newly formed communities, creating a breach that held until 1758 and beyond. This chapter also discusses that historic split, how the Irish experience affected it, and what it meant to these nascent communities in Pennsylvania.

Where They Settled

As the Scots Irish arrived during the eighteenth century, they fit themselves into Pennsylvania's dynamic ethnic and racial patchwork. By the eighteenth century, because of Penn's encouragement of religious and cultural pluralism and his active recruitment of colonists, the colony had become a "mixed multitude" of different European ethnic groups, which, aside from the Scots Irish, included the Dutch, Finnish, and Swedish settlers who were the remnants of the former Delaware Valley colony of New Sweden, many English, Welsh, and Irish Quakers, English Anglicans, some Scots and French, and large numbers of Germans. Enslaved Africans rounded out the mix. Once in Pennsylvania, these newcomers interacted with the many multi-ethnic Indian communities that remained within and near the colony's borders. In a colony characterized by such cultural heterogeneity, the Scots Irish found themselves as one ethnic group among many, a situation quite different from the tripartite social order they had known in Ulster. That meant that they had to negotiate their own place within this throng of humanity.[2]

Popular wisdom holds that the Scots Irish found their place by moving west and settling Pennsylvania's rural interior. While the stories of the Magraws and the McCulloughs confirm that some Scots Irish families had a "predilection for settling in frontier regions," the Scots Irish also built communities in urban and rural settings all across Pennsylvania.[3] The 1790 census documents the pattern; the most densely populated eastern region of the state, which included Philadelphia and the counties east of the Susquehanna River, was 20 percent Scots Irish; central Pennsylvania, which included the Cumberland Valley, was 23 percent Scots Irish; and in the least densely populated western region, which included the growing city of Pittsburgh and its rural hinterlands, the Scots Irish made up 26 percent of the population.[4] By the end of their first seventy years of migration, the Scots Irish had no hold on any single region or place, nor were they an exclusively rural people.

To understand the different kinds of communities the Scots Irish built in Pennsylvania, we begin in the East, with Philadelphia, where plentiful economic opportunities and the city's status as "the unofficial capital of American Presbyterianism" made it an important home for a wide range of Scots Irish immigrants and their descendants.[5]

Irish indentured servants and laboring people, including some Catholics, occupied the bottom rungs of this community; labor demands generated by

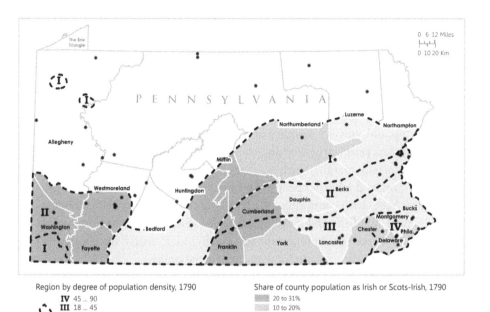

Region by degree of population density, 1790

IV 45 ... 90
III 18 ... 45
II 6 ... 18
I 2 ... 6
Otherwise, less than 2 persons per sq. mile

Share of county population as Irish or Scots-Irish, 1790

20 to 31%
10 to 20%
Less than 10%

* A populated place that shares its name with the Province of Ulster, or a county, barony, parish, or townland in Ulster.

This map shows the distribution and density of the Scots Irish population in Pennsylvania in 1790. The shaded areas show the distribution and density at the time of the first federal census in 1790; the dotted lines set off regions by the degree of national population density (county boundaries are from 1790). Note (1) the settlement of Scots Irish in both densely populated urban and sparsely populated rural areas across the state and (2) the presence of Ulster place names across the state (for more details, see the map featured in the Conclusion). (Map by Scott Drzyzga.)

the city's growing economy had brought them there. Servitude in colonial Pennsylvania was primarily an urban rather than rural phenomenon and by 1731, Philadelphia was the leading market for Irish servants.[6] That meant that male servants from Ireland most often found work in the city's shipyards, ropewalks, and tanneries or in offices and craft or retail shops, while female servants worked as domestics, serving in a range of jobs from governess or seamstress to milkmaid.

Opportunity and necessity motivated many of these laboring people, once freed, to remain in Philadelphia. Since most arrived as young, single adults, many probably hoped to marry and establish families, and the city's expanding Scots Irish population offered them a chance to find partners of the same ethnic and religious background. Former servants also needed work if they were to remain free. In the colony's tight post-1750 wage and labor markets, unskilled laborers had a greater likelihood of finding employment in a city where they had connections and might board cheaply with others, while skilled servants bound to masters in the countryside often relocated to Philadelphia when freed so that they might practice their trade. Despite these opportunities, life in Philadelphia remained challenging for these Scots Irish "lower sorts." The presence of Scots Irish kin and friends and the proximity of the Presbyterian church could not compensate for their lack of property ownership and upward mobility during the eighteenth century. Like other working-class people, the working-class Irish remained economically subsistent and socially marginalized.[7]

Servants and laboring people, however, formed only one layer of Philadelphia's Scots Irish community. Irish immigrants were also well represented in the city's middling and upper social ranks, where they formed the core of a dynamic Scots Irish, predominantly Presbyterian, merchant community that played a leading role in local and provincial politics.

William Allen Jr., the American-born son of an Ulster immigrant, is probably the most extraordinary example of those on the top rung of the city's Scots Irish social ladder. His father, William Allen Sr., had come to America in about 1709, nearly a decade before the first great wave of Ulster emigration began. That early start may have offered some advantages, for he quickly established himself as a merchant, married into a prominent Quaker merchant family, and died a wealthy man in 1725. The son built on his father's success. He married Margaret Hamilton, the daughter of Andrew Hamilton, the politically influential Scots immigrant attorney who won fame in New York for successfully arguing John Peter Zenger's case concerning freedom of the press and later became Speaker of the Pennsylvania Assembly. Thanks to connections pioneered by his father, William Allen Jr. became an extremely wealthy Atlantic World merchant, slave-trader, ironmaster, and land speculator. He founded Allentown and became a powerful politician in the colony, serving as mayor of Philadelphia and a justice on Pennsylvania's Supreme Court. Also, he was a leader of the political faction of "proprietor's men" who supported the leadership of William Penn's son Thomas against Quaker politicians. As with most other Scots Irish, religion was central to his life. Allen was an active member of Philadelphia's First Presbyterian Church and a philanthropist for various Presbyterian causes. As a cultural leader, he was the consummate Philadelphia gentleman; he and his family enjoyed a luxurious life in their Philadelphia town houses and at their country estate of Mt. Airy in Germantown; they traveled in a coach and four and had servants and slaves to meet their needs. Though atypical in the degree of his wealth and influence, Allen nonetheless embodies the pinnacle of what the most well-connected and entrepreneurial Scots Irish families could achieve in colonial Pennsylvania.[8]

Outside Philadelphia, Scots Irish urban life flourished in the many new interior towns founded during the eighteenth century, including Lancaster, Easton, and Carlisle, and later Bedford and Pittsburgh. Much as in Philadelphia, the Scots Irish who settled these towns included first- and second-generation Scots Irish families from a variety of class and occupational backgrounds. Those who did best, however, were generally of middling economic status. They brought education and kin connections with them from Ireland and used these advantages to become "disproportionately active in [these] newer cities and towns," where they often formed the principal leadership class. As building blocks of English imperialism in Ulster, towns were familiar settings to these newcomers, offering them the prospect of safety in numbers when confronted by potentially hostile neighbors, whether the native Irish in Ulster or Indians in Pennsylvania. Since many of these towns were also county seats, they boasted dynamic economies with many opportunities for social and political mobility. Together, such favorable circumstances played to the versatility and entrepreneurship that many Scots Irish colonists valued.[9]

Scots Irish town dwellers took their own unique but still representative paths. Because they did not enjoy the same level of wealth, power, or Atlantic World business connections as their Philadelphia counterparts, they looked to their new communities, or to the frontier, for opportunities for themselves and their families. As the previous chapter shows, men like William Irvine typified the minority who earned social prominence but not great wealth as urban professionals and then military and civil servants. Other men leveraged the resources and associations they had to serve the needs of the rapidly expanding backcountry as tavern keepers, innkeepers, shopkeepers, or artisans, positions they might well have held in Ulster.

Carlisle, the county seat of Cumberland and one of the principal towns west of the river, was full of these men and the businesses they operated with the assistance of their wives and children and sometimes servants or slaves. John McCallister is one example. Although we know nothing of his personal history or family, we know that he kept a tavern from 1751 to 1756 in a large, two-story stone house on one of Carlisle's main streets. With stabling for eighty horses, his business was geared to serve the numerous travelers, migrants, and traders moving through this crossroads place into Pennsylvania's West or the southern backcountry. McCallister was one of many Scots Irish colonists who adapted their ambitions to suit their surroundings.[10]

This drawing of a Lancaster tavern is an example of the substantial structures that some backcountry Scots Irish settlers built to house their businesses. (*Drawing of a Tavern in Lancaster.* Courtesy of LancasterHistory.org, Lancaster, Pennsylvania.)

Many other small-town merchants and shopkeepers, perceiving opportunity in the West, took up a new pursuit and engaged in the fur and skin trade with native peoples. Some Carlisle residents, including McCallister, sold rum and brandy illegally to local native peoples. But many others, including William Irvine's father-in-law, the Irish-born Anglican Robert Callender, engaged in a more systematic and mostly legal trade with the Indians that built on the Scots Irish heritage of intercultural relationships in Ireland, where they had grown accustomed to their position as middlemen between English settlers and Irish natives. Callender was a mill owner, a land speculator, and a trader who launched many trips to into the Ohio Valley during the 1750s and 1760s from his home in Carlisle. By taking the risks associated with these trips, he became a broker in a lucrative trade that connected Indian hunters and trappers to Atlantic World merchants in Philadelphia and Europe, a role that won him status and some economic success. His business also had broad influences on the town and its inhabitants, because he employed local men to haul goods, furs, and skins for him and hired local women, and perhaps some servants, to sew shirts or shifts for trade with Indians.[11]

Because rural life predominated in colonial America, the majority of Scots Irish settlers, like other colonists of the time, settled either in the rural hinterlands of towns or on the frontier, where they established "open-country neighborhoods" of contiguously settled, moderately sized farmsteads with access to creeks, springs, or other water sources.[12] The prospect of landowning drew them to the rural parts of Pennsylvania, but since most of these families had farmed for generations in Scotland and Ireland, farm life was familiar. Where they settled, and whether they purchased lands or squatted, however, was determined by the colony's land policies, their economic resources, their connections to other Scots Irish kin or friends in the colony, and the existence of a Presbyterian meetinghouse. The presence of Indians also affected the choices they made.

Many colonists, including the McCullough family, whose experiences open this chapter, purchased lands through traditional legal means, including sheriffs' sales. Poorer families took advantage of the "long peace" that existed between the colony and native peoples between the 1680s and 1750s and negotiated directly with local Indians to obtain permission to squat on lands not yet possessed by Pennsylvania. They hoped that the labor and improvements they invested in these lands would yield them ownership. Until that happened, however, they lived rough-hewn and precarious lives, interacting regularly, and sometimes uneasily, with nearby multi-ethnic Indian communities while trying to steer clear of provincial authorities who saw their settlements as a challenge to colony authority.[13]

Farming remained the principal occupation of these settlers in the interior, but rural life in Pennsylvania was different from what they had been accustomed to in Ireland. They were more distant from market centers than they had been in rural Ulster, which meant they were more isolated. In response, community rather than individualism took precedence, as settlers cooperated to build networks of communication, production, and trade among themselves and to connect to urban market centers and seaports. Settling in the interior also meant living in close proximity to new and unfamiliar groups whose cultures and languages were markedly different from their own. Indians, in particular, they viewed with wary eyes because of the groups' perceived savagery.[14]

Establishing a farm was also a more arduous process in Pennsylvania than in Ulster. Settlers had to first clear their lands of trees, which were more abundant in America than in long-settled Ireland. Scots Irish colonists, like others, typically removed trees by using the girdling or slash-and-burn techniques they learned from Indians. Then, they had to build their houses and barns. Because the thatched-roof stone cottages of Scotland and Ireland were impractical in America, Scots Irish settlers quickly learned to take advantage of Pennsylvania's abundant wood resources for their dwellings. Although historians dispute whether they were inspired by the cabin-style architecture of the British borderlands or the log-construction techniques pioneered by the early Swedish and Finnish colonists of the Delaware Valley, Scots Irish colonists built modest, V-notched log cabins of rough-hewn, squared timbers for their homes that became ubiquitous on the Appalachian frontier.[15]

Preparing and planting their farm fields required additional adaptation. Initially, Scots Irish families, like other colonists, planted their crops Indian style among girdled trees; neatly plowed fields like those they knew in Ireland came later. They planted familiar food crops, such as potatoes and turnips, as well as new, Indian crops, such as corn, squash, and beans. And though they were accustomed to growing oats and barley in Ireland, in Pennsylvania, where flour was in high demand and whiskey could be sold in both local and distance markets, the settlers grew wheat and rye, which could be milled or distilled. As for livestock, pigs more often took precedence in America, especially on the frontier, because they could be left to forage in the woods. The cattle and sheep that were mainstays of Irish animal husbandry were there but in smaller numbers.[16]

Not everything was different, however, for Scots Irish colonists still raised flax in abundance. Flaxseed was a major export crop to Ireland, and it became

This spinning wheel from Rhode Island circa the eighteenth century is typical of the wheels that many Scots Irish immigrant women used in Pennsylvania to spin flax into linen thread. (Spinning Wheel, Flax. Maker Unknown, possibly eighteenth century. Object ID TE.T01959.000. National Museum of American History, Smithsonian Institution, Washington, D.C. Gift of the Rhode Island Society for the Encouragement of Domestic Industry.)

an important cash crop, especially after 1750. Yet as McCullough's journal entries attest, the Scots Irish in America also spun and wove cloth from the fibers that remained once the seeds were harvested. Flax cards and flax wheels were common in many rural households. In rural Chester County, for example, nearly 60 percent of all households owned some kind of spinning wheel.[17] Scots Irish women were essential to this gender-specific economy, much as they had been in Ireland. Women typically had the job of carding and then spinning the tough flax fibers into thread that could be woven into cloth or sold or bartered to neighbors and they could even earn wages for their labors. Linen production thus "remained a defining feature of migrants' lives," much as it had in Ulster.[18]

What Made Them Distinctive?

In many respects, Scots Irish farm families did what every immigrant group to early Pennsylvania did: they adapted their Old World experiences to their New World circumstances through a process of trial and error. Yet contemporary observers and later historians criticized them for being a poor, lazy, and unproductive people who compared unfavorably to other European ethnic groups of their time, particularly the Germans. Whereas many Pennsylvanians praised German immigrants as model agriculturalists whose neat and highly productive farms aided the colony's growth, these same observers condemned Scots Irish farm families for what they saw as unkempt fields, coarse living conditions, and drunken rowdiness, declaring it all an embarrassment. By the reckoning of these critics, the hardscrabble existence Scots Irish colonists had carved out for themselves in the interior was a cautionary tale of how not to make one's way in early America.[19]

Such critiques fed stereotypes of Scots Irish cultural coarseness and inferiority. During the past half century, however, scholars have done much to challenge these negative portrayals by offering evidence that the Scots Irish were no less capable or successful than other European immigrant groups to early Pennsylvania; nor were Scots Irish farms any less productive than German or English ones. In eighteenth-century Chester and Lancaster Counties, German, English, and Scots Irish farm practices were more alike than different. Members of every ethnic group were to be found settled on both the most and the least fertile lands, where they farmed a mix of oats, corn, flax, hemp, and wheat; all of them also kept pigs. In addition, members of all groups owned slaves. About the only distinguishing feature among them was a minor one: the Scots Irish and English were more likely to keep sheep than were the Germans. Thus, the Scots Irish were not distinguishable by an innate indolence or lack of skill in farming.[20]

Nor were they known for having a unique material culture.[21] Unlike other Pennsylvania groups, such as the Quakers, who marked themselves with their plain speech, simple dress, and broad-brimmed hats, Scots Irish Presbyterians used no distinctive forms of speech or dress to mark their ethnic identity. To be sure, most of them probably spoke with a distinct brogue, and evidence suggests that they added unique, Ulster-derived pronunciations, grammatical forms, and terms to Pennsylvania's lexicon, but these qualities were products of their ethnic heritage and historical experience in Ireland, rather than a self-consciously constructed form of address.[22] Being migrant people had taught them to adopt Anglo clothing styles. In their dress and outward appearances, then, they were mostly indistinguishable from any English man or woman of similar class status. Their houses and domestic furnishings were also influenced by cultural borrowing, but from multiple sources. In America, for example, the Scots Irish accommodated to both local and English architectural precedents. Whereas Pennsylvania's German houses, even the log ones, were notable for their asymmetrical three-room interior floor plans, and for the distinctive craft traditions displayed in the elaborately painted furniture and needle-worked textiles inside these homes, Scots Irish houses and their contents were indistinguishable from others, particularly English ones, in the colony. In building their dwellings, the Scots Irish adapted Old World styles, adopted techniques they encountered in America, or followed English design traditions by building in stone or brick. Because they evidently brought few goods with them from Ulster, they furnished their homes with what they could purchase. In the homes of the less advantaged that meant a mix of modest-range locally made and imported goods. Wealthier families mimicked the lifestyles of English gentlemen and ladies, enjoying the comfort and refinement of higher-end, imported English consumer goods.[23] About the only distinctive Scots Irish material-culture tradition scholars have identified are their gravestone carvings. These elaborate carvings, done by artisans such as the Ulster stonemason William Bigham, who settled in Lancaster County during the late 1730s, favored heraldic themes that reinforced family ancestry and connections to Europe.[24]

What most distinguished the Scots Irish from other European groups in the colony was their Presbyterianism, the religion of the majority of Ulster immigrants, which profoundly affected their attitudes toward and approach to the world.[25] Presbyterians' Calvinist belief system and the representative governing structure of their churches were the most prominent markers of their group identity, which valued faith, discipline, hierarchy, and representative forms of governance. As believers in God's ultimate sovereignty and predestination, Presbyterians placed a high premium on spiritual and social order.

Their spiritual relationship to God was a hierarchical one in which God ruled over humanity. Yet Presbyterians also acknowledged the vital horizontal relationships that existed among them as a community of believers. In Scotland, where Presbyterianism originated and became the state church, lay preferences played a strong role in its evolution. In Ireland, where the Presbyterian minority had to compete with Catholics and the Anglican Church of Ireland, the Presbyterian Church depended on a strong spirit of voluntarism to sustain itself; Irish Presbyterians made a conscious choice to join and remain in the church. These beliefs and experiences translated into a hierarchical and simultaneously intensely communal church in which church governance rested on congregants' choice to grant ecclesiastical authority to specially elected groups of men who would govern in congregational-level sessions, regionally based presbyteries and synods, and, eventually, in the General Assembly of the church.[26]

The church was central to Scots Irish Presbyterian communities and lives. The growing number of Presbyterian meetinghouses, academies, and later colleges dotting Pennsylvania's landscape were the most obvious physical markers of the expanding Presbyterian presence in the colony; these structures anchored the communities they served. The Presbyterian Church also structured congregants' worldviews by emphasizing the importance of faith, piety, and devotion, while demanding that they have knowledge of the Bible and various catechisms, and that they listen to the lengthy sermons of their ministers on the Sabbath. The requirement that they know the Bible placed a high premium on literacy and education. Moral authority within Scots Irish communities and households was also rooted in their Calvinist beliefs and in church-based disciplinary bodies that policed behavior of their congregants. The university-educated ministers who preached to their congregations were among the most highly respected members of their communities.[27]

That organized Presbyterianism actually preceded the major Ulster migration waves of the eighteenth century was a critical factor in making the church central to newcomers' lives. New Jersey and Pennsylvania became "the nexus of colonial Presbyterianism," and the Ulster-born minister Francis Makemie, "the father of American Presbyterianism," was critical to that process.[28] Although he worked primarily in Maryland, on a visit to the new city of Philadelphia in the early 1690s, he gathered together a congregation of Presbyterians; by 1698, they had organized the city's First Presbyterian Church. Makemie was back in the colony in 1706 as one of a small and diverse group of Presbyterian ministers who met in Philadelphia to organize the colonies' first presbytery. After a decade of sustained growth, but while still on the cusp of the first major flow of Ulster immigrants into Pennsylvania, church leaders met again in 1716 to organize the Synod of Philadelphia, the body charged with supervising the three presbyteries then in existence at Long Island, Philadelphia, New Castle, a projected new presbytery to be founded at Snow Hill, Maryland, and an increasing number of congregations. As Ulster immigrants began to arrive in great numbers after 1710, they found a growing American church with a governing structure and seventeen ministers to serve them.[29]

Even so, this church was different from the one these newcomers had known in Ulster. In the religiously tolerant climate of Pennsylvania, Presbyterians were no longer dissenters, which meant that they no longer had to pay tithes to a national church or suffer discrimination, and they had the freedom to worship as they pleased. Yet because ethnic and regional diversity marked the American church in ways it had not in Ulster, American Presbyterianism was a unique and sometimes discordant blend of various Reformed impulses and traditions that balanced faith and doctrine differently than in Ireland; it was a diverse church for a diverse region. For Scots Irish Presbyterians, this situation demanded adaptation. In eastern Pennsylvania particularly, new families from Ulster worshipped alongside English, Scots, Welsh, and sometimes even German or Dutch Reformed peoples. More significant, Ulster Presbyterians' commitment to local autonomy, expressions of dissent, and scripture over man-made creeds and their sometimes flexible attitudes toward orthodoxy were challenged by others in America who pushed for full subscription to the Westminster Confession of Faith, a statement of Calvinist belief adopted in 1646.[30] These circumstances made the process of building the Presbyterian Church in Pennsylvania complicated and sometimes tense, especially in such a rapidly expanding colony where the growth of Ulster immigrants quickly outpaced church growth.

In Philadelphia, Ulster immigrants could worship at First Presbyterian or, after 1743, at the New Side Second Presbyterian. And though these American congregations were ethnically diverse, they were established communities to join. The Ulster immigrants who settled in the interior faced greater challenges. There, congregations were more likely to comprise other Ulster people, but they had to build them. To do so, they first organized themselves into congregations, requested the services of a minister, designated or erected a meetinghouse for their services, and, typically, chose lands for a burial ground. The time required, however, meant that most frontier congregations met initially in someone's home or business before erecting a log structure for their meetings. Their efforts paid off quickly. Many new congregations arose in Philadelphia's hinterlands beginning in the 1710s, and on the eastern and western sides of the Susquehanna by the 1730s; the Presbytery of Donegal followed shortly thereafter in 1732.[31]

This 1800 view of Philadelphia's High Street features the First Presbyterian Church on the right. (*High Street, with the First Presbyterian Church. Philadelphia. Taken down in 1820 / Designed & published by W. Birch enamel painter, 1800.* Hand-Colored Engraving. LC-DIG-pga-05814, Library of Congress, Prints and Photographs Division, Washington, D.C.)

Backcountry Presbyterians typically worshipped in simple log or, as in this instance, stone meetinghouses. (*Exterior of Donegal Presbyterian Church*, Donegal Township, Lancaster County. Courtesy of LancasterHistory.org, Lancaster, Pennsylvania.)

This interior view of Donegal Presbyterian Church, featuring a table, a chair, and four chalices, shows the modest style typical of many early Presbyterian meetinghouses, especially in the backcountry. (*Interior view of Donegal Presbyterian Church,* Donegal Township, Lancaster County. Courtesy of LancasterHistory.org, Lancaster, Pennsylvania.)

Yet settlers faced challenges in making their new congregations fully functional. Some congregations, especially those on Pennsylvania's frontiers, were too small and too poor to support ministers. Other congregations of greater size and resources were unable to hire permanent, salaried ministers because the growth of new congregations outpaced the number of ordained clergy. Because of the severe shortage of ministers in America, itinerant ministers became the mainstays of many congregations.[32]

This "threadbare Presbyterian system" had consequences. With no permanent minister to lead them, some congregants, especially those on the frontier, slid into the chaos of daily lives that were dominated by poverty and uncertainty, hard living and hard work, great quantities of liquor, and threats of violence.[33] Others embraced a self-generated order of their own making. The church's shortage of ministers accorded the laity new opportunities to play vocal roles in governing all aspects of their congregations, which included imposing order by hearing disciplinary cases against their members and, in some instances, by assisting clergy in pushing for uniform subscription to the Westminster Confession.[34]

Awakening and Division

In the midst of this prolonged period of community and church building in Pennsylvania came a new internal challenge posed by those gripped by the evangelical fervor known as the Great Awakening. In the broadest sense, the Great Awakening was a transatlantic religious revival of the long eighteenth century that was marked by the birth of an evangelical form of piety in Western Europe and America that continues today in various modern forms.[35] In the Presbyterian Church, however, the Awakening took a unique form that stemmed from the shortage of ministers but that touched off a much deeper and more divisive quarrel over the tenuous balance between piety and assent to creed. In positioning New Sides (evangelicals who put emphasis on faith and conversion) against Old Sides (those who opposed this evangelical turn), the Awakening tore many of Pennsylvania's congregations and communities asunder.

The origins of the Awakening seem straightforward; it was rooted in efforts to meet the Presbyterian Church's shortage of ministers. In 1727, the Ulster-born Rev. William Tennent, who had received his degree from the University of Edinburgh, founded a school at Neshaminy, Bucks County, to educate Presbyterian youth (boys only) and train them for the ministry. It was a small place, housed in a modest log structure that was located on his lands there. Despite its size, Tennent had ambitious goals for his school. He wished to educate Presbyterian youth and encourage them toward the ministry through a rigorous curriculum of Greek, Latin, theology, and the arts and sciences. His plan worked. By the 1730s, Tennent was graduating a small and steady stream of students from what his detractors called the "Log College." Many of these men, including his three sons, became the advance guard of an American-educated ministry who would serve the many new congregations cropping up in Pennsylvania and elsewhere in the Middle Colonies.[36]

Ministers trained by Tennent had different sensibilities and approaches than many of their European-trained counterparts. Tennent's curriculum was heavily influenced by the rise of a new, transatlantic evangelical religious sensibility that had begun slowly in the late 1600s in England and the colonies and was gaining momentum at the time he founded his college. This sensibility, which built on Presbyterian notions of faith and the centrality of scripture, emphasized a new kind of experience-based religious enthusiasm grounded in the personal spiritual awakening of individual congregants. Ministers who had experienced this conversion and identified themselves with this new sensibility called themselves New Lights or, if they were Presbyterian, New Sides. These clergymen, particularly Tennent, did not reject church orthodoxy, nor

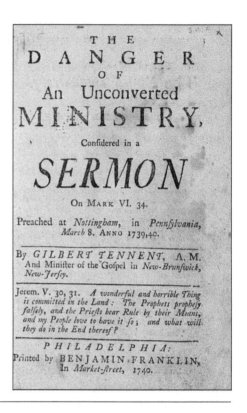

In a now famous sermon, the Reverend Gilbert Tennent urged his fellow Presbyterian clergymen to heed the call of the Great Awakening and convert. (Gilbert Tennent, Benjamin Franklin, and Benjamin Franklin Collection. *The Danger of An Unconverted Ministry, Considered in a Sermon on Mark VI. 34 . . . Philadelphia: Printed by Benjamin Franklin, in Market-street, 1740.* Library of Congress, Washington, D.C., https://www.loc.gov/item/06001773/.)

did they disdain the role of an educated ministry, as some of the most radical practitioners of the Awakening did. Rather, they emphasized that clergy and laypeople both must experience God through conversion. William's son Gilbert offered the strongest expression of these ideals in his famous and widely reprinted 1740 sermon, "On the Danger of an Unconverted Ministry," in which he charges that his unconverted clerical opponents lack a divine call to the ministry and are thus unqualified to preach. To him, as to other proponents of the Awakening, because conversion was the fundamental building block of faith and church, only a converted clergy could inspire this awakening in others by rousing them from complacency.[37]

Tennent's school and its students had profound effects on the American Presbyterian Church, especially in the Middle Colonies, where evangelicalism took off. Tennent's sons, especially Gilbert, were instrumental in spreading the Awakening's messages through their itinerant preaching and published sermons, and they worked cooperatively with other Reformed groups, such as Dutch pietists, to spread their evangelicalism. Other New Siders took the lead in founding additional educational institutions throughout the region, including Samuel Blair's academy at Fagg's Manor and Robert Smith's in Pequea. The most enduring New Side contribution, however, was the founding of the College of New Jersey (now Princeton University) in 1746, which was patterned after Yale and Harvard and designed to be a training ground for American-educated Presbyterian clergy.[38]

While Tennent and others reshaped the Presbyterian Church, other events of this Awakening exerted an equally strong influence over how ordinary Scots Irish Presbyterians in Pennsylvania experienced their religion and pursued salvation. Most notable among them was the American preaching tours of the English Methodist minister George Whitefield, which began in 1739. Whitefield launched his first tour in Philadelphia, by then the second largest city in the colonies, with thirteen thousand people. He drew enormous attention by preaching outdoors in field meetings to huge audiences that sometimes numbered nearly eight thousand. The setting was informal, but his style and message were thunderous. He preached that grace, rather than doctrine, had to transform one's heart before one could achieve salvation. Press coverage and

This photograph shows Nassau Hall, on the campus of Princeton University (formerly the College of New Jersey), in the 1850s. (F. De B. Richards, photographer. [Nassau Hall, Princeton University.] New Jersey, Princeton, None. [Place not identified: publisher not identified, between 1850 and 1855.] Photograph. LOT 14120, no. 39 [P&P]. Library of Congress, Prints and Photographs Division, Washington, D.C.)

word of mouth ensured that those who did not or could not attend his meet-ings heard about them and were affected secondhand. Whitefield was pivotal in stirring bottom-up momentum for this revival.[39]

However powerful the Awakening was to its adherents, it was also a tre-mendously divisive force in Scots Irish religious and community life. A coa-lition of clergy and laypeople, calling themselves Old Sides, arose to oppose it. Scholars long held that the clergy among them were a group of stodgy, Old World conservatives who demanded doctrinal orthodoxy and tried to quash their opponents, but that is not so, especially in Pennsylvania where the Scots Irish had such sway over the church. In actuality, Old Side Scots Irish Pres-byterians were moderates who shared a common Ulster Presbyterian heritage with their New Side rivals. Yet they were unwilling to compromise with the most radical calls from New England–influenced Presbyterians who wanted to de-emphasize the need for an educated ministry. As Irish Presbyterians, they were equally opposed to conservative calls from Scottish Old Sides who demanded American conformity to the Church of Scotland. As their chief spokesman, the Donegal-born Rev. Francis Alison, argued, "Scotland, Ire-land, and American all had different churches and ought not to foist their peculiarities on each other."[40]

By the 1740s, the continuing debate over the Awakening caused a schism between New Sides and Old Sides, splitting the Presbyterian Church into rival synods until 1758. In Pennsylvania, Old Side ministers, though the minority, managed to oust their New Side counterparts from the Synod of Philadelphia in 1741. They adopted Francis Alison's Chester County academy as their own training ground for ministers, and when Alison moved to the newly founded Academy of Philadelphia (eventually the University of Penn-sylvania) in 1752, they shifted their attention to this nondenominational school. The schism also had profound effects on local communities, as con-gregations split apart during the 1740s and, in some instances, remained separate for decades beyond the synodical reunification in 1758. In Philadel-phia, this division resulted in the founding of the New Side church, Second Presbyterian. On the east side of the Susquehanna, in Donegal Township, Lancaster County, Old Sides formed their own congregation, calling John Elder to be their preacher. Farther west of the Susquehanna, in communities that were just being settled as the Awakening began, the split was woven into the developing social fabric, setting precedents for tense social relationships among various Scots Irish families that lasted for decades.[41]

Carlisle offers an instructive example of how intense and long-lived these divisions were. In 1758, the year the church made amends and called on divided congregations to reunite, New Sides from the nearby Meeting House Springs congregation, which dated to 1734, broke from their divided congregation, moved into town, erected a log meetinghouse just south of the square, and installed as their minister Rev. George Duffield, a native of Lancaster who had been educated at the College of New Jersey. Their Old Side counterparts from Meeting House Springs initially stayed in place and installed the Irish-born Rev. John Steel as their new minister. In 1761, however, at Steel's urging, this congregation also moved into town and erected their own frame meetinghouse just north of the square. Their move gave Carlisle two, rival Presbyterian congregations, which co-existed uneasily in the fledgling town. As Duffield wrote, many of the New Sides were "very generally disgusted" by the arrival of the rival church and the appointment of Steel. "Our affairs here look with an aspect as gloomy both in Church & state as when our Indian Enemys infested our Borders."[42] Tension between the two congregations worsened when Steel's Old Sides obtained permission to erect a new meetinghouse on the town's square, the location that Duffield's congregation had once claimed. Steel's congregation then erected the stone structure that remains today and moved into the building in 1770. Although the coming of the American Revolution and the departure of Duffield inspired the two congregations to reunite by 1779, tensions within the community lingered into the 1780s and 1790s.[43]

As the glue that held Pennsylvania's Scots Irish communities together and the belief system that distinguished them from others, Presbyterianism was a vital component of their group identity. Thus, the Great Awakening and the bitter schism it caused had profound effects on the Presbyterian Church, its clergy, and its Scots Irish congregants. In the Delaware Valley, the American home of the church, the bitter split between New Sides and Old Sides caused the two sides to work at cross-purposes in ways that diluted the church's power and its political influence in the colony's capital. In the interior, the Awakening greatly complicated the settlement process, pitting neighbor against neighbor in ways that were not easily repaired, especially when the devastating Indian frontier raids that marked the start of the Seven Years' War in Pennsylvania began during the 1750s. Consequently, the Scots Irish found themselves divided from within and threatened from without. As they moved into the 1760s, as the next chapter shows, that situation had dire consequences.

4

FIGHTING INDIANS AND OTHERS

Those cruel Men . . . suddenly appeared in that town [Lancaster], on the 27th of *December* [1763]. Fifty of them, armed as before, dismounting, went directly to the Work-house, and by Violence broke open the Door, and entered with the utmost Fury in their Countenances.—When the poor Wretches [the Conestoga Indians] saw they had *no Protection* nigh [near], nor could possibly escape, and being without the least Weapon for Defence, they divided into their little Families, the Children clinging to the Parents; they fell on their Knees, protested their Innocence, declared their Love to the *English*, and that, in their whole Lives, they had never done them Injury; and in this Posture they all received the Hatchet!—Men, Women and little Children—were every one inhumanly murdered!—in cold Blood!

The barbarous Men who committed the atrocious Fact, in Defiance of Government, of all Laws human and divine, and to the eternal Disgrace of their Country and Colour, then mounted their Horses, huzza'd in Triumph, as if they had gained a Victory, and rode off—*unmolested!* (Benjamin Franklin, *A Narrative of the Late Massacres, in Lancaster County.* . . . [1764])[1]

WHAT HAD HAPPENED IN LANCASTER on that fateful December day in 1763 when a group of fifty armed frontiersmen rode on horseback into the town, broke open the doors of the town's workhouse, and murdered fourteen unarmed, Christianized Conestoga men, women, and children? Who

This 1841 illustration of the infamous Paxton "massacre"—although factually inaccurate in its depiction of the Paxton men (who are dressed in suits), the Conestogas (who are barely clothed), and the outdoor setting (it took place inside the workhouse, not in the streets)—is the only extant image of the Paxton men's brutal December 1763 attack on the Conestogas in Lancaster. ([Matthias S. Weaver.] *Massacre of the Indians at Lancaster by the Paxton boys in 1763.* 1841. From James Wimer, *Events in Indian History . . .* [Lancaster, Pa., 1841]. The Library Company of Philadelphia.)

were these fifty men? What circumstances prompted their heinous actions? Contemporary writers debated answers to these questions, as do scholars today. Although the identities of these frontiersmen were never revealed because no one was ever arrested for this crime, most scholars agree that the majority of these men came from frontier Lancaster County, specifically Paxton and Donegal Townships, and that frontiersmen from Cumberland County joined them. They were mostly Scots Irish, and many were probably recent immigrants to the colony.[2]

Less clear is why these men acted as they did and whether their heinous actions were justified. Benjamin Franklin's sensational account of what he called the "Paxton Boys massacre" made his position clear. Affirming stereotypes of the Scots Irish as belligerents, he charged that these "CHRISTIAN WHITE SAVAGES of *Packstang* and *Donegall!*" were "Murderers."[3] His pamphlet set off a firestorm of public debate, which led to a pamphlet war between the critics of their actions and those who tried to explain why this group of Scots Irish frontiersmen had committed such an atrocity.[4] This war of words is important for what it revealed about the motives of the group that became known as the Paxton Boys and how this debate became a proxy for a larger discussion about the status and authority of Scots Irish Presbyterians in the colony.

With the Paxton Boys' "massacre" as its launching point, this chapter tackles the provocative topic of Scots Irish cultural violence, particularly as it was directed against Pennsylvania's native peoples during the 1760s. Thanks to the controversial actions of the Paxton men, Scots Irish frontiersmen gained a reputation as virulent Indian haters whose ungovernable passions could destroy the colony. This chapter explores how and why they earned this reputation and assesses whether or not this reputation was deserved.

The End of Peace

Understanding the origins of such intercultural violence calls for an examination of the colony's history at mid-century. The peaceable, culturally diverse colony of William Penn was gone. But what events had triggered such animosity and violence between Scots Irish colonists and Indians?

To begin, we must reconsider popular assumptions of Pennsylvania as an idealized peaceable kingdom and acknowledge the existence of long-standing cultural tensions in the colony's society and politics. By mid-century, Pennsylvania was under stress from many sources. The flood of Scots Irish and German immigrants who had arrived during the eighteenth century was a major source of strain. Since many of these newcomers were on their way into the interior in search of land, they often encroached on Indian territory. Initially, the groups got along. But each group was always wary of the other, and tensions mounted with the arrival of more and more European colonists.[5]

Pennsylvania's colonial leadership, including the proprietors and the officials who oversaw the colony for them, was another source of tension. In juggling their multiple interests in the colony's interior, these men often upset the precarious cultural balance-of-power that existed there between Indians and colonists. As we have seen, in an effort to police native peoples and the colony's Maryland rivals, the provincial secretary, James Logan, had encouraged Ulster immigrants to move west. Yet he had not figured on the strain their presence would create, or how they and their communities would undercut proprietary interests and goals. Tensions mounted after William Penn's son Thomas became the colony's principal proprietor in the early 1730s. Because of his heavy debts, Thomas Penn wanted desperately to make his colony profitable; he also was interested in winning a long-standing border dispute with Maryland that dated to his father's time. To accomplish his goals, he placed great emphasis on the orderly survey and sale of land, the collection of rents, and the regulation of the fur and skin trades on his colony's frontiers, while also demanding settler loyalty in what became a heated border dispute known as the Conojocular War or Cresap's War with Maryland during the

1730s. Poorer Scots Irish families of the interior suffered greatly from Penn's policies, which dramatically undercut squatters' ability to claim lands and disrupted the informal exchange economies of the backcountry. Even worse, these policies encouraged open hostility and violence toward Maryland colonists and Indians of the region.[6]

Yet because Thomas Penn was an Anglican, rather than a Quaker like his father, he also found himself at odds with the colony's Quaker-dominated assembly. That meant he had to rely on a group of like-minded Anglican and Presbyterian "proprietor's men" (agents in the colony who acted on his behalf in exchange for patronage and various perks) led by the wealthy Scots Irish colonist William Allen to carry out his frontier policies. With the goal of preventing this "very Valuable Country" from "being cut to pieces by a Rabble," they evicted squatters, promoted land surveys and purchases, and collected overdue rents. Thus, Penn's policies also divided Pennsylvania's Scots Irish by pitting a group of privileged and politically connected Scots Irish against their less advantaged and often struggling brethren on the colony's frontiers.[7]

Officials used aggressive tactics to enact these policies. Sometimes Scots Irish squatter or tenant families who were evicted from their homes watched as officials, who may have been fellow Scots Irish accompanied by native peoples, then burned their cabins. On at least one occasion in 1750, an angry Scots Irish colonist in Cumberland County brandished a loaded gun and threatened to "shoot the first man that dar[e]d to come nigher [nearer]." Those in charge responded by arresting him and burning his cabin, just as they planned to do.[8]

The Delawares, Shawnees, and other native peoples within or near the colony's borders were also angry. Evicting squatters from their lands was not enough, especially when Thomas Penn double-crossed them by negotiating a 1736 treaty with the Iroquois that gave the Six Nations supremacy over them in exchange for a major land purchase. Although this treaty represented a "major shift" in Pennsylvania's Indian policy, Penn hoped this Iroquois alliance would centralize diplomacy and yield more effective management of his colony. For the Delawares, Shawnees, and others, however, this treaty was a major blow to their autonomy. Their anger then grew the following year when Penn and his officials cheated the eastern Delawares out of their remaining northern Delaware Valley lands in the infamous Walking Purchase of 1737. This "land grab," which added to Pennsylvania an immense tract of land bordering the Delaware River, remained a source of grievance among the Delawares for over two decades, and controversy over it clouded their relationship with the colony.[9]

Despite these tensions within the colony, the intensifying imperial rivalry between Great Britain and France ignited the Seven Years' War, the military conflict that had the most disastrous effects on Pennsylvania and its peoples. Friction between these two European rivals had been building in the Great Lakes and Ohio Valley during the eighteenth century. These tensions came to a head in 1754, when a young George Washington, representing the Ohio Company, bungled his attempts to claim the Ohio Valley for a group of Virginia land speculators; the outcome was a bloody skirmish, a humiliating defeat at the hands of the French and their Indian allies, and an embarrassing surrender for Washington that set the stage for an imperial crisis. War between Britain and France followed in 1756 and quickly evolved into a global conflict of major proportions.[10]

War in Pennsylvania

The outbreak of war was a profound jolt to Pennsylvania and its inhabitants, ending the long peace that had defined Pennsylvania since its founding. The Scots Irish settlers in the interior were among those most disturbed by the war. Between 1755 and 1757, raiding parties of Ohio Valley Indians who were allied with the French terrorized frontier colonists. In these raids, which stretched east as far as Reading, Indians attacked and burned settlements, killed and scalped white colonists, and took many others captive. One historian estimates that five hundred Pennsylvanians were killed or captured during this time.[11] By all reports, the frontier was in chaos. Gruesome accounts of the murder and destruction of colonists, many of them Scots Irish, filled the pages of Philadelphia's newspapers. Penn's Creek, on the west side of the Susquehanna, was the site of one of the worst atrocities in October 1755. Delaware and Shawnee raiders killed and scalped at least thirteen Scots Irish and German colonists there and carried away twenty-eight others as captives.[12]

With floods of refugee colonists arriving in towns such as Carlisle, York, and Shippensburg seeking shelter, Pennsylvania experienced an unprecedented reverse migration. This pattern continued when additional raids threatened those towns and refugees fled again to safer spots east of the river, making the Susquehanna "the western boundary of civilization."[13] Colonists in Cumberland County, Pennsylvania's largest and westernmost county, were said to be in "the greatest Distress and Confusion imaginable." According to reports, "the whole Country to the West" of Carlisle, the county seat, had been "abandoned."[14]

Fearing for their lives, the colonists made repeated appeals to colony officials for arms and ammunition to defend themselves. Yet in a colony where no colonial militia existed and pacifist Quaker assemblymen controlled the purse strings of government, armed defense of the frontier was a hotly contested political issue between the colony's Quaker and Anglican leadership. The upshot was a political standoff that left Pennsylvania's interior colonists defenseless until 1756, when the Pennsylvania Assembly finally allotted monies for defense.[15]

Feeling abandoned by the colony that had encouraged their immigration, frontier colonists took matters into their own hands. They fortified some rural farmsteads as defensive blockhouses.[16] They organized themselves defensively. At first, they formed voluntary groups of rangers. After 1756, they organized militia units with commissioned officers. In Lancaster, two Ulstermen, Adam Read, a farmer, and Thomas McKee, a fur trader, both commissioned as captains, helped lead companies who patrolled rural settlements east of the river.[17] West of the river, in Carlisle, another Ulsterman, John Armstrong, a devout New Side Presbyterian and a proprietor's man, was commissioned a colonel. He was given the challenging task of protecting the expansive colonial settlements on the colony's westernmost edges. But offense rather than defense quickly became Armstrong's primary focus when, with the governor's sanction, he planned an attack and rescue mission on the Delaware village of Kittanning, located about forty miles northeast of Fort Duquesne.[18]

Kittanning had special meaning to many Pennsylvania frontiers people, who believed that Kittanning was the origin point for the most devastating raids on their settlements. It was the home of the Delaware chiefs Shingas and Captain Jacobs. These native warriors had led many of the most destructive raids against colonial settlements, including one on Fort Granville (near present-day Lewiston) in which John Armstrong's brother Edward was killed. Kittanning was also the holding place for many white captives whose families were desperate to free them.[19]

In response, in late summer 1756, Armstrong, along with his second-in-command, the Scots Irish fur trader Robert Callender, the Old Side Presbyterian minister John Steel, and some three hundred men from the local region—many of them Scots Irish too—set off from Carlisle to Kittanning in a raid of retribution and rescue. At dawn on September 7, they staged a surprise attack, killing as many Indians as they could, destroying a cache of ammunition, and laying waste to the village and its farm fields with fire. Pennsylvanians greeted news of the town's destruction with elation. Colony officials hailed the Kittanning expedition as a success and feted Armstrong and his men as heroes at a public celebration in Philadelphia, conferring on Armstrong a sword and belt, land, and cash bounties for the Delaware scalps

Philadelphians awarded Colonel John Armstrong this commemorative medal and a bounty payment for destroying Kittanning, the Delaware Indians' village, and killing Captain Jacobs, their chief, in 1756. Although most historians contend that Colonel Armstrong's raid was a failure, this medal—depicting Armstrong and two men looking on as the log buildings of Kittanning burn, while another man shoots and kills an Indian near the stockade—celebrated it as a heroic victory. (*Medal: Commemorating the Destruction of Kittanning by Col. Armstrong, 8 September 1756 [reverse]*, 1756. America, 18th century. Bronze; diameter: w. 5.1 cm [2 in.]. The Cleveland Museum of Art. Gift of Mr. and Mrs. J. H. Wade 1916.1878.b.)

he and his men returned. The corporation of Philadelphia struck a special commemorative medal to honor their victory, which they awarded to Armstrong and his officers.[20]

Such celebrations denied the expedition's violent realities. The Kittanning raid had not gone according to plan. The Delawares had fought back fiercely, and Captain Jacobs had refused to surrender; he defended his house until Armstrong ordered it burned around him. When Jacobs and his family tried to escape the burning structure, Armstrong's men shot and scalped him, his wife, and his son; nine other Delawares suffered the same fate. The expedition's withdrawal did not go as planned either. Shingas and other refugees fled Kittanning, aided by nearby French troops. Fearing further engagement, Armstrong gave orders for an orderly retreat, but that failed also when his men scattered after a fierce fight with Shingas and other warriors.[21]

The expedition's outcome was also contradictory. The Delaware village lay in ashes and Captain Jacobs was dead. But how many other Delawares had been killed was in dispute; some participants said as few as seven, while others claimed as many as forty or fifty; Armstrong guessed thirty to forty men were dead. Despite outnumbering native warriors three to one, seventeen colonists were killed, thirteen wounded (including Armstrong, who was shot in the shoulder), and nineteen missing in action. Armstrong had also lost his supplies while retreating and had freed only seven white captives. Equally significant, Indian raids against Pennsylvania settlements persisted. Kittanning was not the success Armstrong and the colony claimed it to be.[22]

The most striking characteristic of this expedition is the brutality that Armstrong and his men exhibited during the raid. They burned some Indians alive, killed women and children, and scalped at least nine people. Such cruelty, especially coming from a force made up of many Scots Irish frontiersmen, proved James Logan correct; the Scots Irish could be ferocious defenders of the colony's frontier. Their actions also set troubling precedents for the future by fueling mythic representations of the Scots Irish as vicious fighters that lasted for centuries. Kittanning demonstrated how, when driven by intense fear, frustration, and anger, frontier Scots Irish colonists could hate native peoples enough to kill them and destroy their communities. It foreshadowed what became a pattern of racialized violence that white Americans would later employ repeatedly against Indians.[23]

After this expedition, Scots Irish involvement in the war took new directions. By 1757, as the British Army took more direct control of the fighting war in North America, many Scots Irish colonists turned their attention to local defense. Each of the colony's four interior counties, Cumberland, Lancaster, Berks, and Northampton, maintained informally organized volunteer companies of rangers to protect local settlements. Scots Irish traders, merchants, and retailers, meanwhile, redirected their energies from fighting Indians to supporting the British war effort as suppliers, haulers, and support personnel.[24]

New Hostilities

The British capture of Fort Duquesne in 1758, which the British renamed Fort Pitt, brought peace to Pennsylvania's interior after the years of terror. But that peace did not last for long. A new war with Ohio Valley Indians began in 1763, just after the British declared final victory over the French. Pontiac's War, which was named for the Ottawa chief who led it, was a violent expression of native frustration over British Indian policy. It was inspired by the spiritual teachings of the Delaware prophet Neolin, who argued that native cultural survival depended on pan-Indian unity and a common rejection of British culture. Acting on this frustration and inspiration, Pontiac seized the British-held Fort Detroit. Shawnee, Delaware, and Mingo warriors then launched a new round of raids on Pennsylvania's frontier settlements to express their rejection of British rule.[25]

To war-weary Scots Irish colonists living in Pennsylvania's interior, predictions that native warriors would again cross the Susquehanna were almost too much to bear. As the Presbyterian minister John Elder reported from Paxton Township, Lancaster County, colonists were "quite sunk & dispirited, so that it's to be feared that on any attack of the Enemy, a considerable part of the

Country will be evacuated, as all seem inclinable to seek Safety rather in flight, than in Opposing the Savage Foe."[26] Something had to be done to stem the tide of violence. The Pennsylvania Assembly responded speedily this time. At the governor's behest, they allotted funds and commissioned officers, including John Armstrong in Cumberland County and Rev. Elder in Lancaster to lead defense efforts west and east of the river.[27] The mustering of these defensive forces, however, did little to reassure frontier colonists. In a repeat of the 1750s, rumors of new attacks ran rampant and rural refugees flooded into backcountry towns.

Pontiac's War lasted less than a year, but it still had devastating effects on intercultural relations in Pennsylvania's interior. In rebelling against the British, native peoples scorned colonial officials and colonists. Frontier colonists, many of them Scots Irish, feeling terrorized again, turned to hate. To them, Indians were no longer neighbors or trade partners but violent adversaries whose very existence threatened their own. Thanks to the extended intercultural violence of two wars and the growth of an influential "anti-Indian sublime" that exaggerated Indian misdeeds and colonists' victimization in Pennsylvania's print media, Indian hating united the diverse colonial communities of Pennsylvania's interior, binding them together in ways other events and circumstances had not. Among the Scots Irish, in particular, hatred of Indian "others" coupled with righteous self-defense did much to reconcile families of diverse class and status backgrounds and to repair the spiritual rifts between New and Old Sides from the Great Awakening.[28]

Pontiac's War also brought regional tensions to a head. As Pennsylvania expanded demographically and geographically during the eighteenth century, new stresses arose between the colony's original Quaker settlers in the Delaware Valley and the Scots Irish Presbyterian and German Lutheran and Reformed colonists living in the interior. Politically, interior colonists were underrepresented in the colony's assembly, and this was a sore spot. Ethno-religious tensions existed as well. While Quaker Philadelphians sometimes derided the Scots Irish as frontier ruffians, the Scots Irish perceived the colony's Quaker leaders as greedy and self-interested; they were insulted by Quaker pacifism and they could not understand Quaker beliefs in the common humanity of America's native peoples. To the Paxton men and their supporters, the Quakers seemed to care more about native peoples than they did about the sufferings of their fellow colonists because they were willing to "enslave the Province to Indians" so that they might earn profits from trading rather than warring with them.[29]

Fear and hatred, compounded by a sense of abandonment by provincial and even some local elites, created a volatile combination in Pennsylvania's backwoods. Once again, interior colonists began to take matters into their own hands. But this time, with hundreds of men already organized into local volunteer militias, such as the Paxton (or Paxtang) Rangers and the Cumberland Boys, they had some real force at their disposal. As Pontiac's War concluded, companies of backcountry rangers started to exceed their provincial mandate as defensive forces and began to strike out offensively against native enemies because retaliation was their goal.[30]

The "Massacre" and the Pamphlet War
That Followed

Colonists' hatred came to a head in Lancaster County with the Paxton men's attack on the Conestogas in December 1763. In certain respects, this was a surprising turn of events. Lancaster was not the colony's westernmost county; nor had its settlers borne the brunt of native raids, which were mostly concentrated to the west and north. But news of the brutal destruction of settlements in the upper Susquehanna Valley and firsthand observation of how brutally the Delawares had tortured their victims sparked local fury, compounding local class and ethnic tensions. With a well-organized group at its disposal known as the Paxton Rangers, Lancaster had sufficient men to revenge these losses.[31] And one of their leaders, the Presbyterian minister-turned-militia-captain John Elder, was eager to act in ways that were "encouraging to the frontier inhabitants," including spurring "Young Adventurers" to join expeditions against native enemies.[32]

The brutal retaliatory expeditions staged by a group of these "Young Adventurers"—the infamous Paxton Boys—against the peaceful, Christianized Conestogas of Lancaster provoked a storm of controversy. In the first of the two assaults that would be popularly known as the Paxton "massacre," the men surprised a group of Conestogas who were living in a small hamlet on proprietary manor lands north of Lancaster Town in mid-December 1763. During the raid, they descended on the native village in the early morning hours, killing and scalping the six people they found asleep there. Afterward, they rode back into Lancaster where they "jubilantly paraded the scalps, their trophies of success, through Lancaster, and the townspeople laughed."[33] Although some locals condemned their behavior as "disorderly" and called them "robbers," the Paxton men and their supporters held that their actions were justified. The Conestogas, they asserted, were not peaceful allies of the colony but duplicitous spies who conspired with other native peoples to undermine colonial authority.[34]

The second, even more shocking incident, detailed at the opening of this chapter, occurred several weeks later. By this time, local officials had brought the surviving fourteen Conestogas to Lancaster Town, housing them in the city's workhouse to keep them safe. But their efforts failed. On a day in late December, witnesses watched as another group of Paxton rangers, most of them probable participants in the deadly raid on the Conestogas' village, rode into town on horseback, this time carrying rifles, tomahawks, and knives to signal that they were "equipped for murder."[35] At the workhouse they pushed aside the local authorities who were standing guard, broke through the doors, and murdered and scalped all of the Conestogas housed there, which included three married couples and their eight children. They accomplished these deeds in less than twelve minutes.[36] Sure of their cause and believing that many locals supported these murders, the Paxton men then "got back onto their horses, rode around the Court House, fired their guns repeatedly, screamed and made a horrid amount of noise" in a general effort to "publiciz[e] their feat." The next day, in a testament to the local hatred of Indians, townspeople threw the bodies of the fourteen murdered Conestogas "like dogs" into a large pit, cursing them and saying that the Indians "had it coming to them."[37]

As news of these deeds spread to Philadelphia, colonists and provincial officials reacted with outrage. Governor John Penn issued a proclamation offering a two-hundred-pound reward for the arrest of these men. Outrage turned to fear, however, when news came in early 1764 that some two hundred men from Lancaster County, presumably including many of the same Paxton men who had murdered the Conestogas, had formed themselves into a company and were marching to Philadelphia with the intent of killing another group of approximately 140 Indians, all of them Moravian converts, who were being housed and protected by the colony on an island in the Delaware River.[38] Philadelphians panicked. Governor Penn asked for British troops to protect the Moravian Indians and read the Riot Act. With no militia to call out inside the city, residents, including many Quakers, took up arms to defend themselves from their fellow colonists. But the Lancaster frontiersmen never got there. In early February, they were met at Germantown by a delegation of five men, led by Benjamin Franklin, who represented the colony. After a day of talks in one of the town's taverns, the frontiersmen agreed to call off their march and to draft a list of their grievances instead. Peace returned to the city.[39]

The two-part *Declaration and Remonstrance* that the leaders Matthew Smith and James Gibson submitted to the colony was the Paxton men's response. In these documents, which open with declarations of loyalty to Britain's king, Smith and Gibson justify the attacks and list the Paxton men's

This 1764 cartoon poked fun at Philadelphia's Quakers for taking up arms in violation of their pacifist beliefs to defend their city from the mostly Scots Irish Paxton men. ([Henry Dawkins.] *The Paxton Expedition, Inscribed to the Author of the Farce by HD.* Philadelphia, 1764. The Library Company of Philadelphia.)

complaints against the colony's Indians, its Quaker elites, and the conduct of its politics. These emotional texts gave readers a sense of the helplessness interior colonists had felt since the 1750s, the anger they harbored toward the colony's Quakers, and the indignation they experienced at the "excessive Regard manifested to *Indians* beyond his Majesty's loyal Subjects."[40] The *Remonstrance* also lists the political grievances these frontiersmen had with the colony, including the lack of adequate representation for western counties in the Pennsylvania Assembly, their desire to be treated equally to other British subjects, and their opposition to the policy of sheltering and protecting Indians, which undermined the security of their families, lands, and business interests.[41] The *Declaration and Remonstrance* revealed much about the mindset of Scots Irish frontierspeople. By the 1760s, they were angry, frustrated, and resentful; they had come to condemn Quakers as greedy hypocrites and Indians as inherently savage and corrupt peoples.[42]

Yet thanks to Benjamin Franklin, the *Declaration and Remonstrance* was neither the first nor the last word Pennsylvanians read or heard about the incidents at Lancaster, their causes, or their consequences. As the Paxton men marched to Philadelphia in early 1764, Franklin made his own, highly pas-

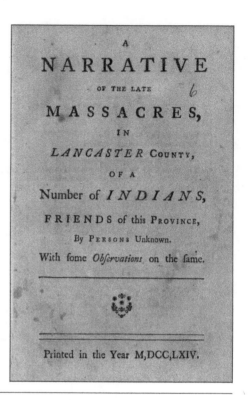

A

NARRATIVE

OF THE LATE

MASSACRES,

IN

LANCASTER County,

OF A

Number of *INDIANS,*

FRIENDS of this Province,

By Persons Unknown.

With some *Obfervations* on the fame.

Printed in the Year M,DCC,LXIV.

Benjamin Franklin's sensational pamphlet placed full blame for the "massacre" of the Conestogas on the predominantly Scots Irish Paxton men. (Benjamin Franklin. *A Narrative of the late Massacres, in Lancaster County, of a Number of Indians, Friends of this Province, by Persons Unknown . . .* [Philadelphia]: Printed [by Franklin & H. Hall?], 1764. The Library Company of Philadelphia.)

sionate appeal with the publication of his incendiary pamphlet. Franklin's work, which opens this chapter, became the inaugural salvo in an intense and highly emotional, year-long pamphlet war in which a small group of Philadelphia authors, editors, cartoonists, and printers hotly debated the Paxton men's actions, using it as a proxy for a broader debate about the political and cultural direction of the colony. In less than a year, they issued sixty-three pamphlets and ten political cartoons.[43]

Franklin set the tone of the debate. Using emotionally powerful language that others involved would imitate, he condemned the Paxton men as cruel savages who had committed inhuman acts in murdering the Conestogas. But Franklin also did something else. In calling attention to the "freckled Face and red Hair" of the perpetrators, he added an ethno-racial dimension to this debate that contributed to building anti-Presbyterian and anti-Irish prejudice among some Pennsylvanians. These Scots Irish Presbyterian frontiersmen, he implied, were different from other colonists, even other Protestant colonists. He doubted their loyalty. As Presbyterians, he argued, they were antimonarchical religious fanatics who were more loyal to their church than their king. More important, because they looked different, he also contended that their physical features were evidence of an inherently violent character. That he then hailed the Turks, the Moors, the Popish Spaniards, and the "Negroes of Africa" as more civil than "these People" made his point all the more powerful to readers of the time; Scots Irish Presbyterians were an inferior breed. As nothing more than bloodthirsty barbarians who acted on the basest, uncontrolled impulses, they were uncivilized, unmanly, and unworthy "others."[44]

In employing these anti-Presbyterian and anti-Irish tropes, Franklin condemned all of the colony's Scots Irish. This rhetorical strategy was consistent with Franklin's political agenda for the colony. During the 1760s, Franklin lobbied hard to oust the Penn family as proprietors and to make Pennsylvania a royal colony; this effort aligned him with many of the colony's most influential Quakers, who were eager to see the Anglican Thomas Penn removed from power. Standing in opposition, however, were many of Pennsylvania's most powerful Scots Irish colonists, most of them Philadelphians, many of them Presbyterians. As Chapter 3 shows, not all Ulster immigrants had moved to the interior. Many of the most privileged and their descendants—men such as William Allen Jr.—remained in Philadelphia, where they became successful merchants and entrepreneurs with strong ties to proprietary authority in the colony. These Scots Irish "proprietor's men" utterly opposed Franklin's efforts. As Presbyterians, they recalled the disadvantages their ancestors had suffered under as dissenters in the British Isles and feared a similar fate would befall them if Pennsylvania became a royal colony.[45]

With this struggle over provincial political leadership in mind, Franklin's published condemnation of the Paxton men must be read as a clever screen for a more targeted strike against his Scots Irish Presbyterian political opponents. And because the province's political fate was at stake in this discussion, other writers joined the fray, fueling a bitter public debate that was more about the "problem of Europeans' prejudice toward one another than on prejudice against Indians."[46] Ignoring the plight of the Conestogas, Paxton critics focused on condemning the Paxton men's actions as virtual treason; as one writer noted, for example, "their design is to humbugg us."[47] These writers also used the discussion of the massacre as a kind of referendum to urge a rollback of the increasing Scots Irish Presbyterian influence in the colony. Following Franklin's example of using long-standing anti-Presbyterian stereotypes to condemn them, these writers reminded readers that Presbyterian loyalty to king and province was questionable. As one wrote, the "Piss-Brute-tarians" [Presbyterians] were a "bigoted, cruel and revengeful sect." As such, this "swarm" of newcomers could not be trusted with the colony's fate.[48]

But not everyone agreed. The Paxton men and the colony's Scots Irish Presbyterian community had defenders who participated just as actively in

In this anti-Franklin cartoon, the helpless "Hibernian" (Scots Irish man) carries a Quaker man on his back and the German carries an Indian, while Benjamin Franklin calls the shots from the sidelines. With a frontier house burning in the background while slain colonists (including a woman and child) lie dead in the foreground, the negative implications of Franklin's control are clear. ([Henry Dawkins.] *The German bleeds & bears ye Furs . . .* , Philadelphia, 1764. The Library Company of Philadelphia.)

the pamphlet war. These writers, few of whom were either Scots Irish or Presbyterian, had their own set of ethno-religious and political motives for writing, and they reframed the debate as a referendum on Quaker dominance in the colony. According to these writers, the Quakers were the real source of the colony's troubles, because members of this sect were nothing more than cold-hearted, self-interested frauds. As one pamphleteer cautioned, the Quakers acted "meek, merciful, [and] compassionate," but they were actually quite wicked. When confronted with news of the frontier attacks of Pontiac's War that had forced "near a thousand Families" from "their Places" of habitation, Philadelphia's Quakers had unsympathetically ignored the plight of the Scots Irish and others on the frontier. These "compassionate and merciful Christians would not grant a single Farthing . . . for the Relief of their Fellow Subjects." But they would assist and even protect and shelter their Indian allies. And that was the rub. The Quakers "cherished and caressed" the Conestogas "as dearest Friends," even after frontier residents accused them of being allied with the colony's "openly avowed imbittered Enemies."[49] For these reasons, Quaker influence in the colony had to be diminished, these writers argued. And though Franklin was not a Quaker, his campaign for royal government had politically aligned him with them. Thus, writers cast Franklin as the colony's biggest fraud; as a shrewd political operator who duped others into serving his own political interests, he was the man really calling the shots.[50]

Aftermath

The fall 1764 elections finally brought an end to the pamphlet war. During that election, thanks to heavy participation by Scots Irish and German voters, Franklin and his Quaker party were mostly ousted from the colony's assembly (at least temporarily). Although the push for royal government continued, the Scots Irish had emerged as a potent political force whose influence would continue to grow in the colony as the American Revolution approached. Most important, though, they had withstood the ethno-religiously based propaganda war waged against them and in doing so had changed the terms of the debate. By recasting their angry violence as a courageous masculine struggle for liberty rather than uncivilized barbarism, the Scots Irish and their defenders claimed their status as men and white Protestants who were equal to, if not superior to, their Anglican or Quaker counterparts. That shift and their presence as leaders of an increasingly powerful Presbyterian party or political faction in the colony suggested that they were there to stay. The Scots Irish had become permanent members of the colony's "mixed multitude."[51]

Yet many other issues remained unresolved, especially on the colony's frontiers. The Paxton men remained at large; none of them was ever captured or tried for the murders they committed. As immigration picked up for a time in the 1760s, newcomers again pushed west on to Indian lands, creating new rounds of tension. This time, however, imperial, rather than provincial, authorities attempted to control the situation with the issuance of the Royal Proclamation of 1763, which prohibited colonial settlement west of the Appalachian Mountains. Their action provoked another western uprising in 1765, this one by the "Black Boys," a group of frontier vigilantes, some of them Scots Irish, who attacked and destroyed a huge wagon train of goods headed to Fort Pitt for trade with the Indians and later waged a two-day siege of Fort Loudon. These frontiersmen, who blackened their faces and imitated Indian guerilla tactics in their raids, saw Indians as a perpetual threat. Yet their goal, unlike that of the Paxton men, was not so much to kill Indians as to teach British imperial authorities a lesson by using a combination of force and terror to halt cross-cultural trade and reshape imperial policy in the region. Quite simply, Indians, rather than loyal Scots Irish colonists, should remain beyond the Pale of settlement.[52]

Thus, as the 1760s drew to close, it was clear that Scots Irish colonists remained antagonistic toward Indians and were willing to take up arms to resist any provincial or imperial policy that imperiled the security of their families, farms, or business interests in the interior. Pennsylvania remained a volatile colony.[53]

5

THE REVOLUTION AND BEYOND

The pleasure I this morning feel of having through the Infinite and kind Redeemers goodness, a life like Mine prolonged Through a long and Severe War, the hardships I have been partaker of, But bless God who has at last given us the Victory, and established our Independancy. Oh happy peace. (Job Johnson, Philadelphia, to Robert Johnson, County Londonderry, Ireland, 1784)[1]

THE AMERICAN REVOLUTION brought opportunities and hardships to Pennsylvania's Scots Irish. For Job Johnson, an unmarried, landless schoolteacher trying to make his way in Chester County, service in the Continental Army offered a chance for upward mobility and adventure. During this "long and Severe War," he spent three years fighting against Indians on the war's western fronts and then joined in the army's defeat of British general Lord Cornwallis at Yorktown in southeastern Virginia. At war's end, he rejoiced in the American victory and thanked God for independence and the return of peace. His reward for service, however, was not the prosperity he had hoped for but "an Ailing Constitution" that kept him bedridden for weeks. Johnson died in 1790 while in only his mid-forties.[2]

Johnson's experiences highlight the paradox of the American Revolution. Its effects were both positive and negative. Even more so than during the Seven Years' War or Pontiac's War, the American Revolution and the protests leading up to it mobilized Pennsylvania's diverse Scots Irish communities by uniting them against a common enemy—Great Britain rather than Indians—and the consequences of that unity were profound. In politics, Philadelphia's Scots Irish joined with their brethren in the interior to usher in a new era of radically egalitarian state politics. In the military arena, privileged Scots Irish stood together with humbler sorts like Job Johnson to fight the British in the East and Indians in the West. The Revolution consequently inspired the Scots Irish to overlook the class, occupational, and regional divides that separated them in Pennsylvania and to join together in a shared identity as Scots Irish American patriots rather than Irish Protestants; as such, the Revolution was an essential vehicle for the group's assimilation and identity formation.

Once the Revolution concluded, however, this unity shattered. Revolutionary ideologies of independence and liberty and a strong commitment to republicanism had raised expectations, but few Pennsylvanians agreed about how the new republic should be constituted and governed to achieve these goals. Which priorities would take precedence? Whose visions of the republic would prevail, and how would it be constituted? Every Scots Irish American harbored an expectation of what the new nation would mean for them, their families, the state, and the nation. But not all could be achieved, and the gap between expectations and realities left a legacy of tension that reopened divisions among them.

This chapter focuses on Scots Irish experience during the revolutionary era, a period broadly defined from the 1760s through 1800. It traces how the Scots Irish united to redefine the state's politics and to make substantial contributions to the fighting war. It then turns to the postwar period to discuss how debates over the new U.S. Constitution and the arrival of United Irish refugees affected these communities. As we shall see, shared wartime experiences united these diverse communities, reformulating Scots Irish identity as ardent patriots. Postwar events tore them asunder once again, however, when debates over the political direction of the state and nation, and the arrival of an even more diverse and politically radical group of "new Irish" immigrants reopened long-standing class and regional divides among them.

The Presbyterian Party Emerges

The 1760s were a tough decade for Pennsylvania's Scots Irish. The violence of Pontiac's War and the issues of defense and political representation triggered among the Scots Irish frontierspeople a brutal backlash against Indians and demands for redress of their political grievances.

Scots Irish Presbyterians perceived the push for royal government led by Benjamin Franklin and the Quaker-dominated Pennsylvania Assembly as a serious threat to their religious liberty. It coincided with a larger struggle to establish an Anglican bishopric in the American colonies that made it all the more ominous. Leading Philadelphia clergymen, such as Francis Alison, a former Old Side minister who co-pastored Philadelphia's First Presbyterian Church and helped lead the College of Philadelphia, opposed both royal government and an American episcopacy, fearing they would be the first steps toward the establishment of Anglicanism as the official church of Pennsylvania. In response, he rallied Scots Irish and German voters to defeat Franklin and his Quaker party in the hotly contested 1764 elections. His success temporarily delayed the possible ouster of the proprietors.[3]

Scots Irish Presbyterians were also among the principal opponents of the 1765 Stamp Act, a British tax levied on all colonial legal documents and newspapers to help finance the administrative costs of their North American colonies. Colonists across America widely opposed this controversial tax, and they successfully resisted its imposition by staging street protests, boycotting British goods, drafting resolves, and endorsing the meeting of the Stamp Act Congress that submitted a collective declaration of grievances to Parliament. In the midst of this furor, however, Pennsylvanians generally stood out for their "prudent, peaceful, dutiful, and submissive behavior."[4] Such quiet moderation was the work of Philadelphia's leading Quakers and Anglicans who offered little opposition to the tax because they feared mob rule and offenses against the British ministry.

The response of these men left a coalition of other city leaders, many of them Scots Irish Presbyterians, to take the lead as the Stamp Act's principal opponents. Scots Irish frontiersmen may have been preoccupied with Indian hating and vigilante border policing in the West during the mid-1760s, but their urban counterparts were not. With an imperial crisis brewing, these Philadelphians fixed their gaze across the Atlantic to Great Britain. During first the Stamp Act crisis, and later during the multiple contests over British authority that followed in the 1760s and 1770s, these men mobilized in ways not seen before. Their actions transformed the loose coalition that was the "Proprietary Party" into the more politically coherent Presbyterian Party, which was eager to confront British claims to power over issues of taxation, representation, and a possible American episcopacy.[5] Their rise to power had profound effects on Pennsylvania's revolutionary era politics. As David Doyle notes, "The nascent American nationalism of the region became heavily Presbyterian in tone, and Ulster leaders took a leading role in attempting to brow-beat recalcitrant Quaker and Anglican merchants into compliance with the non-importation movement of 1765, of 1767 . . . , and again of 1770 and after."[6]

Although this new party was not exclusively Scots Irish or Presbyterian (the Englishmen John Dickinson, Timothy Matlack, and Charles Wilson Peale were also leaders), an assemblage of Irish Philadelphians (most of them Scots Irish) was among its vanguard. These men included two immigrants: George Bryan, the wealthy Dublin-born Presbyterian merchant whose fierce commitment to embargoes as a means of protesting British imperial coercion would drive him into bankruptcy, and Rev. Francis Alison, who was instrumental in mobilizing Presbyterian clergy behind the American cause. Also among them were two of Alison's students, including another immigrant, the Londonderry (Derry)–born Charles Thomson, a teacher and merchant of middling means who was active in the city's Sons of Liberty and who would serve as secretary of the Continental Congress, and the Chester County–born son of Ulster immigrants, Thomas McKean, an attorney who would sign the Declaration of Independence and later serve as chief justice and governor of Pennsylvania.

Uniting these men was their common ethno-religious heritage and their vital intellectual grounding in the Scottish "moral sense" philosophy of Francis Hutcheson. According to the Irish-born and Glasgow-educated Hutcheson, man's virtue rested on an innate and universal "moral sense" that could be honed to triumph over selfishness and promote public benevolence and private morality. In practice, that meant Hutcheson placed a high premium on relatively equitable divisions of property, widespread access to education, religious freedom, and the necessity of broadly representative forms of government. With his bold assertion that "all government exists for the good of the governed," Hutcheson's theories were also applicable to more radical defenses of English liberties for all in Ireland and America.[7]

In America, Alison, who was the de facto intellectual leader of the Presbyterian Party until his death in 1779, was instrumental in conveying Hutcheson's ideas across the Atlantic and instilling them in the minds of the state's revolutionary vanguard. Alison was a Hutcheson student and a virtual conduit of his ideas. As an enormously important educator, first at his Old Side New London Academy and then at the College of Philadelphia, Alison read Hutcheson's "moral sense" philosophy to his Pennsylvania students. Yet he also put what David Doyle characterizes as his own "Ulster bluntness" on his mentor's philosophies, arguing that "the end of all civil power is the public happiness, & any power not conducive to this is unjust & the People who gave it may Justly abolish it."[8] Taking "moral sense" philosophy to heart as they galvanized support against the arbitrary and unjust authority of the British during the 1760s and 1770s, Presbyterian Party stalwarts translated Hutcheson's ideas into a political radicalism that supported fundamental

The son of Ulster immigrants, Thomas McKean (1734–1817) rose to become an influential state and national political figure during the revolutionary era and later served three terms as the state's Democratic-Republican governor (1799–1808). (*Thomas McKean.* Charles Willson Peale, after 1787. Oil on canvas. National Portrait Gallery, Smithsonian Institution. Gift of Mary Buchanan Redwood.)

change in the colonies' imperial relationship with Great Britain and set the stage for revolution.

In more practical terms, the Presbyterian Party gained strength because its leaders used the prerevolutionary committee system to bypass the colony's conservative assembly. Their political radicalism had broad appeal in culturally diverse Pennsylvania, a colony where, as Chapter 4 shows, not all ethno-religious groups or classes had equal access to political power. Working at the grassroots in Philadelphia to build momentum for resistance, the party initially found considerable support within the city's artisan and laboring classes, particularly among those of Irish, English, and German ancestries.[9] Yet the party's base of support widened considerably beyond Philadelphia when news of the Coercive Acts (punitive measures Britain targeted at Boston as punishment for the Tea Party) spread anti-British outrage into the backcountry in 1774. When the Presbyterian Party called on county leaders to bypass the Pennsylvania Assembly and form their own Committees of Correspondence and volunteer militias to coordinate local actions and express their support for Boston, interior Pennsylvanians, privileged and poor alike, flocked to the resistance movement. Presbyterian Party radicalism had effectively tapped Scots Irish, English, and German colonists' suspicions of British authority and their provincial complaints over lack of political representation and Quaker dominance of the colony. In calling for local self-governance and policing, party stalwarts had unleashed an equally "powerful idea of rule by the people."[10] In Cumberland County, locals gathered at Carlisle's First Presbyterian Church and drafted resolves supporting Boston, the creation of a continental congress, and more boycotts of British goods. They chose a thirteen-member Committee of Correspondence from among the county's leading men; this committee, which soon morphed into a Committee of Observation to oversee local affairs, was predominantly Presbyterian and included a sizable proportion of Ulster or Scots immigrants (William Irvine and the Scots immigrant James Wilson were among them).[11]

The rise of the Presbyterian Party and the coming of the Revolution motivated Pennsylvania's Scots Irish colonists to put aside their geographical and class differences and unite around a common opposition to Great Britain. As leaders of the state's resistance movement, these religious dissenters and immigrants had found their means to assimilate to American culture.

Revolutionary Politics in Action

The Scots Irish faced new challenges once the war began and colonists declared their independence. Fighting for American nationhood was a high-stakes gamble that demanded unprecedented levels of leadership and commitment. To have any chance of success, the new United States needed military as well as political leaders, a critical mass of men willing to fight for the Continental Army and in various militia units, and a committed citizenry—men and women both—who were willing to support the cause through production and sacrifice. In Pennsylvania, the Revolution took a unique turn. Independence finally resolved the divisive debates over the colony's governance by abruptly ending the Penn family's proprietorship, while the outbreak of war prompted the withdrawal of pacifist Quakers and German sectarian peoples from politics. These major changes opened a political-power vacuum that Scots Irish of all socioeconomic status levels eagerly filled by volunteering for various kinds of political and military service. By the mid-1770s, Pennsylvania's Scots Irish saw a dramatic reversal of their political fortunes; rather than struggling to gain political influence from the colony's social and geographical margins as they had been doing for decades, they and their Presbyterian Party were now among the groups at the center of power in the new state.

In politics, "honest and well meaning [Scots Irish Presbyterian] Country men" of more limited economic means, with less education and experience in government, joined leading Philadelphia Presbyterians to become the state's revolutionary vanguard.[12] These Presbyterian radicals, with help from Reformed Germans, sparked a dramatic internal revolution by writing a new state constitution that restructured the state's political and social order. This 1776 constitution, which historians agree was the most radically democratic plan of any adopted by the new states during the Revolution, shifted power away from the Quaker and Anglican elite who had long dominated the colony to a more inclusive segment of the population. With popular sovereignty as one of their guiding principles, the state's revolutionary leadership wrote a new constitution that aimed to overturn the old eastern-centered and Quaker-dominated order. They made voting more widespread; all free male taxpayers and their sons over twenty-one could vote, not just property holders. Also for the first time, Pennsylvania's more numerous interior and western counties were fully represented in the assembly, giving interior parts of the state a clear numerical advantage over the Philadelphia region. Still, the hallmark of this innovative new government was its annually elected, unicameral assembly, which its creators vested with executive and legislative powers. With representatives restricted to serving for only four years out of seven, with a rotating president and weak council as its nominal head, and with the courts subject to legislative influence, the new Pennsylvania Assembly reigned supreme. The only check on the new government was a weak Council of Censors that could review the actions of the legislature.

Yet because the Scots Irish radicals also believed that the Revolution posed threats from enemies within, they passed the Test Acts to force conformity and ensure allegiance to the new state government; consequently, all political participants and office holders and any man wishing to bear arms, sit on a jury, or buy or sell land was required to swear loyalty oaths. These highly undemocratic measures, which drew the kind of exclusionary lines that bore striking similarity to the hated Penal Laws that the English had imposed on Irish Catholics and Scots Presbyterians in Ireland, effectively disenfranchised Quakers and other pacifist sects who refused to swear oaths, along with neutrals and Loyalists. The Scots Irish radicals compounded the penalty by taxing those who refused the oaths more heavily and restricting their access to courts and commerce. With this one measure, Scots Irish revolutionaries had transformed Pennsylvania's government and emasculated their political opponents, particularly their much-loathed neighbors, the Quakers.[13]

Such change did not come without considerable tumult, because not all of Pennsylvania's revolutionaries supported the radical turn of the 1776 constitution. As Owen S. Ireland notes, between 1776 and 1778 Pennsylvania's politics was in chaos as "patriots fought patriots for control of the new government and the British invaded the state and occupied the capital."[14] The outcome by 1779 was a political split that produced two pro-revolutionary parties. On the radical side stood the majority of Scots Irish Presbyterians and their German Reformed allies, who formed the core of the new Constitutionalist Party. As their name implies, they staunchly defended the new constitution and the rigorous enforcement of the Test Acts, which helped to keep them in power; they also defended the remaking of the College of Philadelphia into the Presbyterian-dominated University of Pennsylvania. They were opposed by the Republicans, or anti-Constitutionalists, a coalition of Anglicans, Quakers, Lutherans, and some Scots Irish Presbyterians and Irish Catholics, all of them moderates and some of them former Presbyterian Party adherents who opposed the excesses of the new government. These men hated the way the new constitution concentrated power in the hands of the legislature. They cautioned moderation in the enforcement of the Test Acts and opposed the restructuring of the College of Philadelphia.[15]

Despite these divisions and the tensions they generated, the shared goals of winning the Revolution and governing the state during the crisis of war bound these two groups together until the end of the war in 1782, when the Republicans swept into power and animosities resurfaced again.

Pennsylvania's Scots Irish also played major roles in fighting the war, forming the backbone of the state's Continental Army and militia units. "Nearly half the Revolutionary War soldiers who fought in the Continental army and state militia units raised in Pennsylvania were of Irish birth or descent, and in some companies (as of the seventh regiment) the proportion was as high as 75 percent."[16] Beginning in 1775, central and western Pennsylvanians led the state in volunteering. That spring, just after the war's first battles at Lexington and Concord, some three thousand Cumberland County men—many of them Scots Irish, others German, some English—stepped up as volunteers in the state militia; five hundred of them were organized to march at the first emergency call. Others volunteered to lead these units; John Montgomery of Carlisle commanded the Flying Camp, a group of early responders, and John Armstrong, the leader of the infamous 1756 Kittanning expedition, having achieved the rank of major general, commanded the entire Pennsylvania militia.[17]

Large numbers of Scots Irishmen signed up for service in the Continental Army too. Central and western Pennsylvanians were again among the earliest and most enthusiastic volunteers, and many remained for the duration of the war. The First Pennsylvania Regiment, known as Thompson's Rifle Battalion, was commanded by the Irish-born William Thompson of Carlisle; it helped to defend Boston during the summer of 1775. After being sent to assist in the invasion of Canada, Thompson and his troops were captured by the British, and he sat out the rest of the war as a paroled but unexchanged prisoner. The Sixth Pennsylvania, which was later reconstituted as the Seventh Pennsylvania, was also organized in Cumberland County. The immigrant physician and former British naval surgeon William Irvine commanded this tight-knit group, which counted Scots Irish Protestants and Irish Catholics among its ranks. Irvine wrote of the "fine fellows" in his battalion, while men such as the Irish Catholic Francis O'Hara declared their loyalty to him by declaring they would "enlist with no other." This battalion also defended Boston and fought in Canada, where many, including Irvine, were captured. But since Irvine was exchanged, he and his men went on to serve in the battles for New York City, New Jersey, and Philadelphia; many of them also served on the western front, including Irvine, who was appointed commander of Fort Pitt in 1781.[18]

Thompson and Irvine commanded three of the seven Continental battalions that were led by Scots Irish from Cumberland County. These battalions, whose rank and file also included many Scots Irish, "fought from Quebec to Charleston and served until Yorktown and beyond" and thus represent an extraordinary pattern of service.[19] Other Scots Irish, such as Ephraim Blaine, another Ulster-born Cumberland County man who became the army's commissary general, served the army in various supportive functions. What motives explain the extraordinary willingness of large numbers of Pennsylvania's Scots Irish to risk their lives in service to America?

The answers are complicated. Ideology played some part. Educated officers, such as Irvine, who had attended Trinity College in Dublin, probably shared an understanding of the Scots Enlightenment ideals that undergirded the Presbyterian Party's political actions and the Commonwealth ideology held dear by many American Whigs. Yet with prior experience in the British Navy, he chose military rather than political service to the cause. Patriotism was also a strong motivator. Scots Irish officers and enlisted men alike expressed a "patriotic Spirit & a readiness to Serve" to protect American liberty. Although patriotism was by no means limited to the Scots Irish, theirs may have had an added intensity fueled by their experiences with the British in Ulster. As one Scots Irish private from William Thompson's Rifle Battalion stated, the Revolution was a fight "to defend the rights of the then colonies against the encroachments of the British Parliament," suggesting that for some this may have been a defensive war against a familiar foe. Because so many of Pennsylvania's Scots Irish were immigrants, military service to the American cause was also an important vehicle of their assimilation; defending their new country offered them claim to an American identity. As patriots who were willing to fight for the cause, they proved their manhood and gained a chance for advancement through military service; officers received military titles, which helped to cement their status as American gentlemen, while enlisted men like Job Johnson hoped for land bounties or greater access to opportunity and public participation.[20]

Racism and revenge were also strong motivators for military service, especially among the Scots Irish of the interior. Coming as the Revolution did during an era when race and hate often formed the dividing line between whites and Indians, the Revolution's frontier war offered the Scots Irish the chance to consolidate their identity as white Americans by joining with other Euro-Americans to fight and kill a common nonwhite enemy. In this way, racism and violence functioned again as expressions of a somewhat warped kind of cultural assimilation, much as they had during the 1760s. Warfare against Indians was also about settling old scores. For many frontier militiamen, soldiers, and some officers, fighting for American independence offered the excuse to finally destroy the native peoples of Pennsylvania and the Ohio Valley, as they had intended during the 1760s.[21] Job Johnson, whose letter to his brother opens this chapter, spent three years "out against the Indians in the Western Army." They were "Savage people that we had to fight against." Still, "the Battles [and] Skirmishes with them and the numbers slaine, with the hardship undergone by us While in their Country, I must not fall on, as it would swell My letter that I would writ[e] Nothing else."[22] These were often brutal fights. Nonetheless, as Gregory Knouff notes, many frontiersmen were "always willing to go on campaigns against the homes of hostile Indians," because they saw "these attacks as honorable, even brave" assaults on what they perceived to be a savage enemy. Thus, much as in the Kittanning expedition, not even the murder of Indian civilians, the scalping and mutilation of Indian bodies, or the destruction of Indian villages and fields were off-limits.[23]

Nor were neutral or friendly native peoples spared the slaughter. In what became "the most infamous example of the indiscriminate racism and total war fought by Pennsylvania frontier soldiers," a group of militiamen, some of them Scots Irish, stationed at Fort Pitt attacked and brutally murdered ninety-six neutral Delawares, Unamis, and Munsees (including men, women, and children) living at Gnadenhutten, a small Moravian mission village along the Muskingum River, in present-day Ohio, in 1782.[24] The goal of this attack, which was led by the western Pennsylvanian colonel David Williamson, was to revenge the murder of frontier settlers in the region. Its victims, however, were Christianized Moravian Indians who lived peacefully and had even offered food and intelligence to officers at Fort Pitt during the war. In actions that were eerily reminiscent of the Paxton men's murder of the Conestogas at Lancaster in 1763, Williamson and his men held a mock trial, condemned these Indian men, women, and children to death, and then beat them with wooden mallets and scalped them in what came to be known as the "Gnaden-hutten Massacre."[25]

To many scholars, this brutal attack exemplified the intense hatred that frontier settlers, particularly the Scots Irish, felt toward native peoples. As Gregory Knouff summarizes, the violence at Gnadenhutten marked "the apotheosis of 'white' racialist identity and the brutalization of frontier war."[26] That those who participated in it openly and proudly claimed their actions and did not hide behind the cloak of anonymity as the Paxton men did suggests the extent to which Indians had become "permanent enemies of the state." Williamson, the expedition's leader, was even promoted for his actions.[27] Nonetheless, not all Scots Irish sanctioned such viciousness; eastern officials, western Continental army officers, including Irvine at Fort Pitt, and the British were all shocked by this turn of events. Their reactions hint at the continuing gap that separated the more privileged, educated, and cosmopolitan Scots Irish leaders of the Revolution from the middling and poorer Scots Irish frontiersmen who actually fought it.[28] This gulf makes it all the more puzzling why authorities did so little to prosecute these militiamen for murder. Irvine even backed off from the investigation and began to embrace some of the racist views he had found abhorrent. The question is why? Pennsylvania's government had certainly changed; with the Revolution, state leaders had become committed to securing borders through the use of force against enemy others. Because of that shift, expediency may have transformed Irvine's revulsion into resignation. He may also have feared alienation from the men in his charge. His lack of action, however, meant that the men went unprosecuted. His response was highly pragmatic and serves as a reminder of how flexible the Scots Irish could be when weighing their options and making choices, even when some of those choices may have challenged their own ethical or moral principles.[29]

Whatever their motives for fighting, because the Scots Irish as a group were so heavily represented in the state's militia and army units, they paid a heavy price for their service. Job Johnson, for example, whose service began with the New Jersey campaigns and ended with the British surrender at Yorktown, got "through the whole without loss of Life, or Members" and rejoiced in America's victory but was left sickly and unable to relocate to the new lands he had acquired in Kentucky.[30] Pension applications, in which veterans describe their selfless service and the battle wounds with which they continue to suffer, reveal that military service left permanent marks on the lives of many men and their families. One soldier, Thomas McFall, was shot in the leg and held prisoner for nearly five months in the battles near Fort Washington. Decades later, his pension claim reports, "his wound yet remains open and deprives him of support by labor." Men like McFall lost a critical claim to manhood when their disabilities left them dependent for survival on small military pensions and the labors of their wives and children.[31]

With a war on and many men gone off to fight, the Revolution disrupted daily life across the state and brought suffering also to civilians. For a year, the British occupied Philadelphia. In the interior, large numbers of settlers lived in fear of attacks by Indians or Loyalists. The economy was in disarray; shortages of goods and cash were common. For Irvine, the war meant extended absences from his young wife, Ann (or Nancy as she was often called), and his growing family. During his war-long career as a Continental officer, he wrote her many emotional letters expressing his longing for her and their children. In one letter, near the end of the war, while he was in command at Fort Pitt, he declared, "I do not intend to live another year apart, whether in, or out of service."[32] At home, Ann Irvine was left mostly alone to care for children and manage servants and the family's home and business interests while her husband was away; like many other women, she did so during repeated pregnancies or while caring for newborns. Postwar county court petitions reveal snippets of the stories of women of humbler means whose husbands were killed in service. In 1787, Margaret McFarland asked the Cumberland County justices for "Support of herself and her infant family." As she explained, her husband, Andrew, a militia captain, had died in 1777 of a "Pestilential fever" while fighting at Monmouth, leaving her with "a number" of small children who were unable to support themselves; she requested that the court grant her a widow's pension, which they did.[33]

The Post-revolutionary Order

The American Revolution had united Pennsylvania's Scots Irish in opposition to the British and their Loyalist and Indian allies. Once the war concluded and the new American nation embarked on the task of defining itself in peace, this collective sense of purpose shattered, and Scots Irish group identity fragmented again. Divisions born of class differences resurfaced, as did the regional divide between urban easterners and rural westerners. After emigration from Ulster resumed in a major way again, immigrants stood out from the native born once more.

The Revolution had mostly shut down the flow of newcomers to the colonies, but in the decades between 1780 and 1830, "many more Ulster Presbyterians (along with other, Catholic Irish immigrants) left Ireland for the United States than had journeyed to Britain's North American colonies in the one hundred years prior to 1776."[34] One estimate suggests that as many as 150,000 Irish emigrants may have crossed the Atlantic between the 1780s and 1814, many of them arriving in Pennsylvania, which remained their principal destination until approximately 1800 when New York City took over. The arrival of so many Ulster immigrants so quickly had dramatic effects; by 1800, at least 12 percent of Philadelphia's residents were Irish born.[35]

These "new Irish" immigrants, however, were different from their colonial predecessors. With the disruption of the lucrative Irish-American trade after American independence, the gradual demise of indentured servitude, and the rise of wage labor in the United States, Irish immigrants arrived as free people in even greater numbers than they had in the past. As such, they were more likely to be farmers and artisans of middling means, or even professionals; they more often emigrated in family groups, and they typically arrived with literacy and perhaps some capital too. More significant, a sizable minority of them were Catholics from outside of Ulster, and they, too, were often from educated families of middling means. Mathew Carey, a printer, bookseller, and newspaper publisher, exemplifies this group. A Dublin-born Catholic, Carey fled to Philadelphia in 1784 after Irish authorities declared one of his newspaper editorials seditious and threatened him with prosecution. Most of all, whether Protestant or Catholic, from Ulster or elsewhere, these postwar Irish immigrants had celebrated the American victory against the British from afar and thus arrived with high expectations of economic achievement and political participation in the new republic.[36]

In another contrast with the past, these immigrants included political exiles and refugees. Inspired by the American and French Revolutions and fueled by the republican ideologies circulating about the Atlantic World in the late eighteenth century, Irish nationalism spiked during the 1780s and 1790s, led by a group of radical reformers from Belfast and later Dublin who founded the Society of United Irishmen in 1791. As their name implies, the United Irishmen included a nonsectarian mix of Protestants, particularly Ulster Presbyterians, and Catholics. Initially, they were reformist in intent but soon committed themselves to fighting their own war for independence from Britain with help from the French. Their goal was to found an independent Irish republic based on universal suffrage for all men, regardless of religion. Their plans for a new Ireland came to naught, however, when a French naval invasion of Ireland in 1796 was aborted because of poor weather, and after the mass uprising that took place in Ireland's Southeast, Northwest, and West in 1798 (often called the Rebellion of 1798) collapsed. The British crackdown was swift and violent. United Irish leaders were jailed; some of them were then exiled or escaped to the United States. Many rank-and-file participants also fled to the United States. For all of those involved, British repression, especially when coupled with the 1800 Act of Union that incorporated Ireland into the United Kingdom, dashed any remaining hopes they had for republican reform and interdenominational unity at home. And so they set their sights on Philadelphia, which large numbers of them chose as their new home during the 1790s and early 1800s.[37]

The Pennsylvania these "new Irish" immigrants entered did not always meet their expectations. Although some, like Carey, found economic opportunity in the city's expanding print trades, early republican politics were far more contentious than most expected.[38] This situation posed a dilemma for all Irish, both newcomers and established settlers, who were "predisposed . . . to see political issues of the period in somewhat starker terms than other Americans."[39] At the state level, the radical revolution of 1776 had given way to a conservative backlash that fractured the tenuous radical coalition that had held authority during the war. Many Pennsylvania Irish, including George Bryan, remained in the radical camp, still committed to the ideals and vision of the more egalitarian future they held as ideal. They were joined in their beliefs by many new immigrants, including former United Irishmen, who brought their own fierce brand of Irish nationalism and republicanism and hatred of the British to the fore. But there were divisions. Some of the more privileged and better connected Scots Irish, including Thomas McKean, defected from the radicals to join the Anglican-dominated coalition of moderates and conservatives who called themselves Republicans. The English-born merchant Robert Morris and two Presbyterians, James Wilson and the physician Benjamin Rush, were leaders of this largely Philadelphia-centered group who dominated state politics during the 1780s and 1790s. These men were ardent critics of the state's wartime government and constitution, and they fought on multiple fronts to undermine the radicals' hold on state politics and minimize the influence of newly arrived Irish radicals.[40]

Republicans lobbied hard to scrap the 1776 constitution and the much-hated Test Acts and to begin anew. Their first step was to relax the Test Acts in 1785. Then, with the impetus of the new U.S. Constitution behind them, they rewrote the state constitution in 1790. Under the moderate plan they designed, the state moved to an elected bicameral legislature, a single governor with limited veto power, an independent judiciary, and a declaration of rights to ensure the liberties of the people. Once the Test Acts were repealed and no loyalty oath was required for voting or office holding, Quakers, German sectarians, Roman Catholics, and even Jews were either re-enfranchised or enfranchised for the first time. Scots Irish radicals fumed at these changes, which were a repudiation of their wartime leadership of the state. The Republicans, by contrast, celebrated.[41]

Scots Irish Republicans also fought a culture war against their radical opponents by founding colleges. Scots Irish Presbyterians believed that "education was the mark of a man," and therefore the founding of schools often followed the establishment of communities and congregations.[42] As the founding of the New Side Log College and the College of New Jersey during the Great Awakening and the contentious battle for control of the College of Philadelphia during the Revolution had proved, overseeing the education of Presbyterian youth was a cause worth fighting over, because colleges were significant forces of cultural and political change. And thus, as the Revolution concluded in the early 1780s, a group of Republicans, led by Benjamin Rush and his Scots Irish friend John Montgomery from Carlisle, formerly an Old Side Presbyterian, began working behind the scenes to found a new, more conservative western college to be located at Carlisle that would teach the state's youth the politics of restraint. Their goal, Rush wrote, was to "rescue the state from the hands of tyrants, fools, and traitors"[43]

In 1783, in response to their efforts, the Pennsylvania legislature chartered Dickinson College. The college, which was named for the conservative politician John Dickinson, who had made a liberal financial contribution to its founding, was the first institution of higher learning located west of the Susquehanna River and one of sixteen colleges that opened in the United States between 1776 and 1800. Although it was technically nondenominational and partly publicly funded, with Presbyterians dominating its board of trustees, and the well-known and conservative Scots Presbyterian theologian Charles Nisbet as its first principal, Rush and Montgomery had virtually ensured that Dickinson College would attract Scots Irish Presbyterian youth from the state's interior. Its seal, which includes a cap of liberty and a telescope above an open Bible accompanied by the motto *Pietate et Doctrina tuta libertas* (Religion and learning, the bulwark of liberty), symbolizes the vision of its founders, who viewed the college as a republican experiment in education and politics. As Rush explained, by serving as "a nursery of religion and learning" in the interior, Dickinson would "school the minds of a rising generation to promote the real welfare of this State."[44]

Although Dickinson College was founded in 1783, the main building, West College—designed by Benjamin Henry Latrobe, architect of the U.S. Capitol—was not built until 1805. (*West College, 1811*. Benjamin Tanner, from a sketch by Alexander Brackenridge. Engraving. *Port Folio*, 5, March 1811. Courtesy of Archives and Special Collections, Dickinson College, Carlisle, Pennsylvania.)

Because Philadelphia was the home of the Continental and Confederation Congresses from 1774 to 1789, and the nation's capital from 1790 to 1800, national politics also had a profound influence on the state. Among the earliest and most contentious issues to confront the state was the ratification of the new U.S. Constitution. Although Pennsylvania was the second state and the first large one to ratify it, the ratification process re-opened old ethno-religious and urban-rural political divides that had originated in the colonial period and come to a head during the Paxton crisis of the 1760s.

On one side of the debate stood the state's Republicans, who were among the vanguard of American political leaders calling for a stronger national government. These men, who supported ratification as Federalists, were mostly Anglicans, Quakers, Lutherans, and German sectarians. Unlike in the 1760s, however, this time they also counted Scots Presbyterians such as James Wilson and some Scots Irish Presbyterian moderates such as Thomas McKean among their ranks. These Scots and Scots Irish Federalists were mostly urban residents whose business interests were aligned with those of the nation (such as the Ulster-born Philadelphia merchant James Caldwell) or Continental Army officers (such as William Irvine) whose military service gave them new claims to authority on the national stage. Ensuring that the nation's future was orderly, stable, and prosperous was paramount to these men.[45]

On the other side of this ethno-religious political divide stood Pennsylvania's Anti-Federalists, a vocal minority of Constitutional opponents who tried to obstruct ratification at the state convention. Scots Irish Presbyterians dominated their ranks, and many of the state's Reformed Germans joined them as allies. These Anti-Federalists, who were mostly rural dwellers of modest economic means from the state's interior, self-identified as defenders of democratic egalitarianism against the continued threats of aristocracy and tyranny. Two of their leaders, the American-born Robert Whitehill, a Cumberland County farmer, and the Ulster-born William Findley, a teacher, weaver, tailor, and farmer from Westmoreland County, exemplified the group's socioeconomic and regional profiles and the deeply suspicious worldview of its adherents. Yet there were exceptions, including the former Presbyterian Party leader and merchant George Bryan and his son. Experiences in Ireland and Pennsylvania had taught Whitehill, Findley, and Bryan to be wary of political power concentrated in the hands of a landed and commercial ascendancy, while their heritage as dissenter radicals bolstered their oppositional stance. They argued that the Constitution, with its emphasis on national over states' rights and the broad tax and military powers it accorded to the new government, represented a conspiracy to reestablish the rule of the colonial elite at the expense of ordinary people like them. In a series of *Centinel* essays, George Bryan's son, Samuel, codified these arguments, lashing out at the wealthy, calling for more equitable divisions of property, and warning against the corrupting influences of consolidated power.[46] The message was clear: the Constitution had to be stopped.

When blocking ratification proved to be difficult, however, because Anti-Federalists were in the minority at the state ratifying convention, Whitehill and Findley took another tack; they insisted on amendments to the plan, which Whitehill outlined in a fourteen-point dissent signed by twenty-one members of the minority. This list, which later served as a model for the Bill of Rights, demanded guarantees for basic civil liberties, such as freedom of conscience, trial by jury, and the right to keep and bear arms for hunting; it also called for broader measures to protect state sovereignty, including stricter separation of powers among the branches, more open elections of Congress, and a watchfulness over the judiciary.[47] As Whitehill summarized, "It is our duty to employ the present opportunity in stipulating such restrictions as are best calculated to protect us from oppression and slavery."[48] To Whitehill and other Anti-Federalists, this meant a government that had little authority over the states, which put Wilson and other Federalists on the defensive. In the end, although Federalists got their way and ratified the Constitution, the objections voiced by the Anti-Federalists ensured that there would be a bill of rights. Pennsylvania's Scots Irish, however divided they were over these issues, left their mark on the nation.[49]

Finishing Out the Century

By the 1790s, with the ratification and implementation of the new U.S. Constitution and a new, moderate constitution for Pennsylvania, the fate of the new American republic and Pennsylvania seemed secure. Yet political strife in the state did not cease, nor did Scots Irish political radicalism. Continuing domestic disputes over the legacy of the Revolution at the national and state levels, compounded by a series of foreign policy crises provoked by the French Revolution and the European war that followed it, inspired the rise of highly partisan, sometimes violent brand of American politics that re-ignited Scots Irish political radicalism during the 1790s.

The first spark occurred in 1794 when western Pennsylvanians, frustrated over a federally imposed excise tax on distilled spirits, undertook a violent agrarian uprising known as the Whiskey Rebellion. Southwestern Pennsylvania was growing rapidly during the last quarter of the century, thanks to a postwar influx of Scots Irish, English, and German settlers; it was fast becoming highly stratified too. Some settlers who arrived in the region with connections, capital, or credit found quick success by founding towns, building mills, and running ferries, iron works, and stores; they formed themselves into a "'mushroom aristocracy'" that dominated local politics. Most settlers, however, remained poor to middling farm families who distilled some of the grain they grew into whiskey to supplement their meager incomes. They had little political voice, though they leaned toward more radical forms of republicanism. Thus, when Congress passed a 25 percent excise tax on whiskey in 1791, a provision of Alexander Hamilton's effort to offset the costs of federal assumption of state debts from the Revolution, these already frustrated western Pennsylvania farmers were driven to protest their disempowered status.[50]

Using words and deeds borrowed from the Revolution, they first refused to pay the tax. They then harassed excisemen and destroyed the stills of larger producers to prevent enforcement. When federal officials threatened them with prosecution in 1794, their protests turned violent. After erecting liberty or "whiskey" poles, they attacked the homes, barns, and even churches of local powerbrokers and anyone associated with the tax. Several thousand marched on Pittsburgh and threatened the federal arsenal there; even more men met on Braddock's field and talked of declaring independence from the

United States. President George Washington, faced with what he and other state and federal officials perceived as an insurrection, responded by sending peace commissioners to negotiate with protestors. He then commanded them to disperse, and finally, he called up a militia army of twelve thousand to defeat them. As he rode west with these troops, the uprising crumbled.[51]

As the "frontier epilogue to the American Revolution," the Whiskey Rebellion was a pivotal episode in the history of the new nation and Pennsylvania because it demonstrated both change and continuity with the past. On one hand, federal and local officials' response to the uprising showed how closely the preservation of order was tied to the perpetuity of the new federal union, especially in the minds of Federalists. On the other hand, western protestors' focus on taxes and tyranny rather than Indians, showed how much things had changed after the U.S. Army's defeat of Ohio Valley native peoples at the Battle of Fallen Timbers in 1794. With the state's western borders secure and the fear of Indians finally gone, interior residents focused their attention on economic issues. Using the rhetoric and tactics of the Revolution as their weapons, they acted to expose the disenchantment they felt about the limits and continued inequities of the new republic.[52]

The Whiskey Rebellion was also a watershed for the state's Scots Irish, who were participants on both sides of the uprising. This event demonstrated the potential radical power of inclusive and united action by Irish citizens (mostly Scots Irish Presbyterians but also some Catholics) to change the republic while also revealing the multiple fractures within this diverse group, which would lead some to more cautious, even critical, responses. Many of the Scots Irish farmers who opposed the whiskey tax were Revolutionary War veterans and Anti-Federalists who rose up to defend their communities against the injustices of a federal government and the tyranny of a wealthy elite. Joining them were "new Irish" immigrants of the postwar period, many of whom sympathized with the United Irishmen and had carried their own "radical-republican or ultra-democratic political ideals" with them from Ireland to America. Together, these native-born and immigrant Scots Irish acted from the grassroots to express their vision for a more egalitarian and participatory republic. Although their uprising failed, their fierce republicanism, with its clear ties to Irish experience, helped to make the Whiskey Rebellion a trans-Atlantic event that pointed to shared hopes of a new more inclusive, democratic future for all and, more immediately, paved the way for Pennsylvania to become a bastion of Democratic-Republicanism by 1800.[53]

Many other Scots Irish, particularly the native born, opposed the whiskey insurgents. These wealthier, more privileged men had also served in the Revolutionary War, but as statesmen and military officers rather than rank-and-file soldiers. They were political moderates during the war, and Federalists who supported the Constitution after the war. Forming themselves into a "nascent Ulster American bourgeoisie" during the early republic, they assimilated to America by rejecting any kind of disorderly behavior that was associated with seemingly uncivilized peoples such as Irish Catholics, Irish radicals, Indians, or the "lower sorts." With the preservation of their social respectability and political authority as their goals, they opposed this uprising.[54]

Presbyterian clergymen, such as Robert Davidson, pastor of Carlisle's First Presbyterian Church, supported their calls for moderation. The sermon he preached on the eve of the troops' departure west stood as a reminder that for many Scots Irish Presbyterians, the "Freedom and Happiness of the United States of America" rested no longer on "tumults and insurrections" but on the peaceful preservation of social and political order. "The Divine Being," he said, "[has displayed] great goodness . . . to our state and nation in particular [for which we owe him] gratitude [and the duty to make] wise improvement [of the] high privileges [given to us]." Not everyone can be equal, he reminded his audience; that is "impossible." Yet, he continued, all Pennsylvanians, especially Scots Irish Presbyterians, should take solace in recalling that America's "infant settlements" have grown so rapidly because those who settled them "were in general a sober, industrious, and pious people." He pointed out that Pennsylvania and the new United States, "one of the most free and excellent [nations] under the sun," needed that kind of sobriety, industry, and piety to ensure their future success. "Unhappy the people who can have no change in their government but what they must obtain by the sword." The Whiskey Rebellion had to end because it threatened the greater good of the nation and its Scots Irish citizens.[55]

Thus, at the close of the eighteenth century, Pennsylvania's Scots Irish were divided once again. Opposition to British tyranny and commitment to American independence had unified them during the war years and inspired ordinary men such as Job Johnson and privileged men such as William Irvine to volunteer their services to the cause. Yet once the war concluded, divisions based in a combination of class status and birthright, as well as connections to Ireland, resurfaced because some found great opportunity awaiting them in the new state and nation, while others did not.

CONCLUSION

Their Varied Legacy

THE NATIVIST RIOTS that swept through some of Philadelphia's Irish Catholic immigrant neighborhoods during the spring and summer of 1844 shocked the city. Racial and ethnic violence was not new to Philadelphia; the city had witnessed a surge of violence during the 1830s that was capped by the burning of the newly built Pennsylvania Hall by an anti-abolitionist, racist mob in 1838.[1] Still, the "massive and prolonged" riots of 1844 were exceptional.[2] This extended wave of white-on-white violence, which pitted native-born Protestants, many of them of Scots Irish ancestry, against their Irish Catholic immigrant neighbors, began in May and was re-ignited in July. It was sparked by Catholic objections to the use of the Protestant King James Bible in the public schools. During these outbreaks, mobs of Protestants, armed with guns, bricks, stones, bottles, and even cannon, descended on the streets of the city's working-class, immigrant neighborhoods and attacked Catholic homes and churches. The city's Catholics fought back. The outcome was "some of the bloodiest rioting of the antebellum period," with at least thirty people killed. It was only the intervention of hundreds of militiamen, policemen, and even some U.S. troops that brought a final end to the violence and restored an uneasy order to the city.[3]

Philadelphia's nativist riots provide a puzzling and troubling bookend to the history of Pennsylvania's Scots Irish. The Scots Irish had earned a reputation for cultural violence, but during the colonial and revolutionary periods that violence had been directed generally against Indians rather than other Euro-Americans. More significant, the Ulster Protestant migrations of the eighteenth cen-

RIOT IN PHILADELPHIA
JULY 7ᵗʰ 1844.

This illustration, depicting a scene following a renewal of nativist rioting against Catholic, predominantly Irish, immigrants in July 1844, shows Pennsylvania militiamen battling well-dressed rioters (presumably including many American Scots Irish Protestants) on the streets of Philadelphia's Southwark neighborhood as women and children flee. Note the similarities to the *Massacre of the Indians at Lancaster* illustration in Chapter 4, which was sketched three years earlier. (*Riot in Philadelphia, July 7th, 1844.* Print. HSP Medium Graphics Collection [V64], Historical Society of Pennsylvania.)

tury had been part of a larger Irish diaspora that had always included some Catholics. For a long time, then, the label "Irish" did not distinguish between Protestant and Catholic. What had happened? What had changed between 1800 and 1844 to inspire such hatred of Irish Catholics among the native-born descendants of eighteenth-century Scots Irish immigrants? Why had these Protestant Pennsylvanians come to be so resentful and angry toward these Irish Catholic newcomers, whom they no longer saw as their own kind?

In 1800, few Pennsylvanians would have predicted such ethnic violence. For Pennsylvania's Scots Irish, there was much to celebrate. Immigration continued, though the majority of Scots Irish, like other state residents, were native born and claimed the new country as their homeland. Also, 90 percent of the residents of Pennsylvania were small-scale farmers who grew wheat and corn and raised cattle and sheep. For Scots Irish families, this meant that they had obtained ownership or access to the land their immigrant ancestors had so coveted. The Scots Irish had also benefited from the state's continued urban growth.

The population of the state's capital city, Philadelphia, continued to grow, increasing from just over thirty thousand in 1774 to just over forty-two thousand in 1790; it would reach nearly a hundred thousand by 1840. The scope and range of the city's commercial enterprises was also widening. Kensington, one of the northeast city neighborhoods most affected by the 1844 riots, was shifting from an economy of fishing and shipbuilding to one of iron, steel, and textile manufacture. In the West, although Pittsburgh was still a small town in 1800, river access to the Mississippi was transforming it into a vital commercial and export center for the interior. Many of its residents were Scots Irish.[4]

In politics the situation looked even more favorable. Persistent Scots Irish Anglophobia, nurtured by the pro-British foreign policies and anti-immigrant domestic policies of the Federalists, had driven the state's Scots Irish en masse to the Democratic-Republican Party during the late 1790s; consequently, they were united once again. They had even more cause for celebration in 1800 when their candidate, Thomas Jefferson, won election as the nation's third president. First under his leadership and then during the presidencies of his fellow Virginians James Madison and James Monroe, the Democratic-Republicans enjoyed a twenty-four-year-long political ascendency. Jefferson's victory coincided with more political good news for Pennsylvania's Democratic-Republicans when, in 1799, Thomas McKean, a moderate Democratic-Republican, won election as the state's governor in what one scholar calls "a Scotch-Irish encore!"[5] He was succeeded by another more radical-leaning Democratic-Republican, Simon Snyder, the son of German immigrants. Together, McKean and Snyder cemented the party's leadership in the state from 1799 until 1817, closed the door on Pennsylvania's Federalists, and ensured that "friend[s] of the people" rather than "lordly aristocrats" were in charge. Thus, in 1800, the state's Irish—Protestants and Catholics both—were empowered by Democratic-Republicanism and united in their commitment to civil and religious liberties in the state and nation. "A synthetic yet legitimate Irish American culture" seemed to have taken root.[6]

As in the past, however, with no external threat or enemy to solidify it, Scots Irish political unity did not last. Political parties were new and tenuous creations in the early republic, and in a state like Pennsylvania, where the Democratic-Republicans represented a coalition of multiple interests and groups, certain "centrifugal tendencies" resurfaced among them "almost immediately" after the Federalists' defeat in 1799. Consequently, they split "into two mutually exclusive camps each of which despised the other."[7] On one side of the divide stood McKean and his moderate-to-conservative followers. By 1805, they had aligned themselves with the state's dwindling number of Federalists to form the Constitutional Republicans, popularly known as the

"Quids." On the other side were the more radical, democratic-leaning follow- ers of Simon Snyder, many of whom wanted to amend the state constitution again and reform the judiciary to grant more power to the people.[8] Although such factionalism was certainly not new to Pennsylvania's Scot Irish, the highly vindictive and personal forms these divisions took during the 1800s foreshadowed the intense class, ethnic, and racial partisanship of the Jackso- nian era. During those years, Andrew Jackson became the most famous Scots Irish American in the United States and the epitome of the kind of ruthless assertiveness and exclusive identity politics that characterized the age.[9]

Fluctuations in the state's economy compounded the political divide, set- ting the stage for ethnic conflict. In the two decades after the War of 1812, the state's economy, like the nation's, had become volatile; commerce and in- dustry were growing, but periodic contractions generated major panics and recessions. In the countryside, residents' relationship to land and agriculture was changing as the state's population continued to expand and its urban manufacturing and commercial economies spread west. The relocation of the state capital to Harrisburg in 1812 and the incorporation of Pittsburgh as a city in 1816 were two measures of this change.[10] Farming remained the eco- nomic mainstay of many Scots Irish families and others, but as manufactories of various sorts opened in small towns across the state, these businesses offered rural dwellers, especially young people, including women, the chance to sup- plement farm income with wage labor. Then there was land, the commodity that had drawn so many Scots Irish immigrants to Pennsylvania. In a state that had been settled for over a century, land was becoming increasingly costly and difficult to acquire. This meant that if Scots Irish families wanted more land for themselves or their children, they had to look west or south to acquire it. And that is what many of them did. Following the pattern of their ancestors in Scotland and Ireland and of earlier Scots Irish migrants who had left Penn- sylvania in the eighteenth century in search of cheaper lands in Virginia's Shenandoah Valley or the Carolina backcountries, they packed up their lives and belongings and migrated into the Northwest Territory or into Kentucky or Tennessee or into the newly acquired lands of the Louisiana Purchase. In doing so, they left Pennsylvania behind, erasing almost all traces of the Scots Irish from many places in the eastern and central parts of the state.[11]

Philadelphia, the state's principal city, exemplified the transformations taking place across the state. Its economy continued to grow during the first half of the nineteenth century, but this growth was unlike that of the past. Philadelphia was no longer the nation's largest city or its principal port; it had lost that distinction to New York City, where the opening of the Erie Canal in 1825 had sealed that city's status as the financial center of the United

States. Baltimore's rise as a port had also impacted Philadelphia by undercutting the Delaware Valley exports of wheat, flour, and other farm products. Still, Philadelphia's economy did not suffer much, because the rise of steam-powered textile production and metal fabrication industries had made it "the most highly industrialized city in the nation" by the 1840s.[12] As such, Philadelphia remained a mecca of opportunity, investment, and wealth for some, much as it had been during the eighteenth century. Yet for the low-skilled wage workers, including the city's Scots Irish working class and the growing number of Irish Catholic immigrants who labored in its factories and dwelled in its densest and poorest neighborhoods, city life meant hardship and deprivation.[13]

Philadelphia was also a ground zero for the myriad cultural changes affecting the state and nation. While fierce anti-Indian prejudice had pitted Scots Irish against Quakers, thereby dividing white, Euro-American colonists during the 1760s, racial issues tied to slavery were the most divisive political and moral issues facing the United States by the 1820s. At this time, anti–African American prejudice fostered a heightened race consciousness among white Americans that tended to unify rather than divide them. Most white Philadelphians, including its Scots Irish, felt these tensions acutely. As "the southernmost northern city," Philadelphia was attracting a growing population of free African Americans and had been since the Revolution. Their presence reminded residents of the growing racial diversity of their city and placed a new cultural premium on the whiteness of European ancestry. It also personified the widening political gap between North and South.[14]

More important to the Scots Irish was the city's and the state's growing ethnic diversity. Irish emigration was on the rise again after 1815. The conclusion of the Napoleonic Wars in Europe in 1815 had prompted a severe contraction of the Irish economy; prices had fallen, industries had collapsed, and unemployment and poverty were on the rise. A series of poor harvests caused by bad weather had set off famines among southern Ireland's predominantly Catholic populace by 1820, inspiring a steep rise in emigration between 1815 and 1844. These emigrants, however, were unlike their predecessors. In a foreshadowing of the mid-century Famine migration, a sizable minority of them were Catholics who saw themselves as exiles for whom migration "represented the only hope of escape from absolute destitution."[15] They arrived in Philadelphia as free people who would become wage laborers rather than servants, but they were poorer and generally less skilled than the Ulster Protestant migrants who had preceded them the century before.

These political shifts and economic transformations, accompanied by the arrival of a major wave of Catholic Irish immigrants, posed choices for the state's nineteenth-century native-born Scots Irish. Pennsylvania was not the same place that their ancestors had immigrated to during the eighteenth century; everything seemed to be in flux. Yet, as in the past, how they responded to the circumstances of the antebellum United States they were a part of depended on their personal backgrounds and circumstances. The Scots Irish remained as they always had been—a diverse people in their class, educational, and occupational backgrounds whose Presbyterianism and political commitment to the American republic united them as a people.

For the most privileged among them, the state's, and particularly Philadelphia's, economic turn to manufacturing, and the transport and banking revolutions that supported it, offered many new opportunities for investment, entrepreneurship, and upward mobility. Even the best-educated and most privileged Irish newcomers, such as Mathew Carey, found numerous business opportunities in Philadelphia and elsewhere in the state. These men, most of whom were Protestant (generally Presbyterian) but a few of whom were Catholic like Carey, rejected radicalism and embraced a politically moderate economic nationalism that included protectionism, internal improvements, and the expansion of the nation's banking system, key features of the Whig Party's platform by the 1830s and important measures of their assimilation into the U.S. political mainstream.[16] Since most were Protestant, the era of renewed religious evangelicalism known as the Second Great Awakening further sealed their cultural identity as Americans and confirmed their moral and social authority in the state and nation. By the 1840s, having achieved the political harmony and social stability that they and their ancestors had sought in Ireland and America, these Scots Irish and their families had "made it" as Americans and Pennsylvanians; they were American success stories.

That brings us back to Philadelphia and its nativist riots of 1844. Scots Irish participation in those riots suggests that differences in class, status, and attitude continued to separate the most privileged Scots Irish families from their less advantaged, less educated, and less skilled Scots Irish neighbors in Philadelphia and elsewhere around the state. To be sure, lower or working-class Scots Irish families enjoyed some advantages. They were American citizens, after all; the men among them took great pride in participating in the political process as voters; they also had their white European ancestry and their Protestantism on their side, weighty cultural factors that gave them a boost in antebellum society.

Their lives, however, were not easy, and they faced many challenges. In the countryside, although Indians were mostly gone from the state, their removal had not made land cheaper or more available; for those families who did not already own land, acquiring it remained difficult. In the state's towns and especially in Philadelphia, the city where ethnic tensions flared so dramatically in 1844, wage labor offered these men, and sometimes their wives and children, new forms of income, but wages were low, jobs were hard, hours were long, and native-born Scots Irish workers faced competition from free African Americans and Irish Catholic immigrants. Their white race and their Protestantism separated them from others in the city, but as the riots of 1844 demonstrated, they also felt under siege and in need of defending themselves. To do so, they acted, lashing out against perceived enemies much as their forebears had done and took to the streets of Philadelphia. Unlike in the past, however, these urban sorts consciously shed their status as "Irish" men and women and proudly and boldly proclaimed themselves to be "Scotch-Irish" Americans as a way to defend their identity as Protestant Irish Americans who were and would remain vital parts of the polity. Thus, the "people with no name" had finally and firmly chosen their own distinctive label, but it was a reactionary one driven by the desire to formalize their status as Americans while "set[ting] themselves apart from an Irish-America redefined as Catholic."[17]

Assessing Their Influence

So, in the end, with Philadelphia's nativist riots in mind, how do we assess the long-term legacy of Pennsylvania's Scots Irish? Who were these people, and what impact did they have on the state and nation?

The "who" question is perhaps the easiest one to tackle. As this book has argued, the Scots Irish were a diverse immigrant group that included families from a variety of class, educational, and occupational backgrounds who arrived in Pennsylvania with often starkly different goals and ambitions. In America, many of those differences persisted, making the Scots Irish a people who could be found in Pennsylvania's cities and towns and in the rural countryside; they were not the exclusively impoverished, ignorant, frontier dwellers popular portrayals have made them out to be. Rather, as farmers, artisans, teachers, ministers, businessmen, and entrepreneurs; as soldiers, vigilantes, Indian fighters, and political and military leaders; and as family members, church members, and citizens, the Scots Irish—men and women—were a diverse group who made a variety of distinctive contributions to their communities, the state, and the nation.

In the economy, the Scots Irish Pennsylvanians were known for their entrepreneurship and their strong desire to succeed. Having been driven from Ireland by various economic hardships, they arrived in America with the intent to stay, and they worked hard to make their way here. Rural families worked cooperatively to farm and trade and to weave flax into linen and distill grain into whiskey. In Pennsylvania's many small towns, Scots Irish formed the cadre of the local leadership class, while many others, with help from their wives and children, operated inns, taverns, and other retail businesses. And in cities like Philadelphia and later Pittsburgh, Scots Irish were among the leading members of the professional and commercial classes and they filled out the ranks of the cities' laboring poor; they worked from top to bottom to take advantage of the opportunities these cities offered them.

Scots Irish distinctiveness was more evident in Pennsylvania's politics. Thanks to their experiences in Ireland as ethnic outsiders and dissenters from the established Church of Ireland, which had left them with an acute sense of the rights and privileges they were entitled to as British subjects, the Scots Irish were committed, sometimes even radical, republicans. They were staunch defenders of religious pluralism, strong believers in the rule of law and the importance of education, and forceful advocates for participatory forms of governance. As such, they played critical roles as state political leaders beginning with the American Revolution and consistently demonstrated their willingness to fight against any enemy, whether Indians, the British, or other Americans, who threatened their cherished values. For these reasons, it is no surprise that the Scots Irish Democratic president, Andrew Jackson, the man who epitomized the birth of participatory democracy with the expansion of the franchise to all white men, came to symbolize the political potential of Scots Irish Americans.

Their cultural contributions to the state, however, remain the most elusive. Because the Scots Irish assimilated so effectively while also remaining a migratory people, their cultural legacy is sometimes hard to see and even more difficult to assess. In today's Pennsylvania, where only 1.1 percent (about 145,000 people) of current state residents identify their ancestry as Scots Irish, the Scots Irish have become virtually invisible as a people, lost amid the tide of global immigrants who have been changing the face of the state since the 1960s.[18] If we look more closely, however, the Scots Irish are still there, their presence observable on the state's landscape and in its culture.

The Presbyterian Church continues to be a powerful entity in the state. The current Synod of the Trinity (once the Synod of Philadelphia) remains the oldest and one of the largest synods in the church.[19] We also see the legacy of the state's first Scots Irish Presbyterian communities in the many stone or brick meetinghouses that dot the landscape; stopping for a quick visit, we note the distinctive Scots Irish names and heraldic themes on the carved gravestones in church cemeteries.[20] The Scots Irish Presbyterian commitment to liberal arts education has also left an enduring mark on the state and its

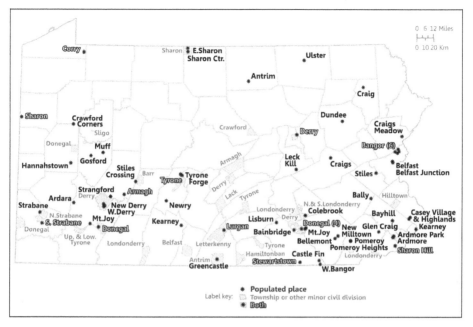

This present-day map shows Ulster place names across Pennsylvania. The Scots Irish named many Pennsylvania villages, towns, and townships after places they had known in Ulster. Today these names (and the places they represent) are important reminders of Scots Irish influence on Pennsylvania's early history and the continuing legacy of the Scots Irish across the state. (Map by Scott Drzyzga.)

residents in the many colleges the Scots Irish founded, from Arcadia University in the East, to Dickinson and Wilson Colleges in central Pennsylvania, to Waynesburg and Westminster Colleges in the West. We see them, too, in the central squares of many grid-planned towns in the central and western parts of the state, where, following Ulster tradition, these market squares are still called "diamonds."[21] And we hear subtle traces of their Ulster Scots dialect when we encounter western Pennsylvanians who address us as "you'ns" and might talk of their potatoes being "boilt" and their ancestors of having lived in "cabins."[22]

The greatest cultural legacy of the Scots Irish, however, may well be the impact they had and continue to have on regions outside Pennsylvania. With Pennsylvania as the "cradle" of their settlement, these migratory peoples took to the road during the eighteenth and nineteenth centuries, fanning themselves out by way of the Great Wagon Road into the southern backcountries of Virginia, the Carolinas, and Georgia, and following other overland routes across the Appalachian Mountains to pioneer the American Midwest, and states such as Kentucky and Tennessee. Once in these new places, they repeated what they had done first in Ireland and then in Pennsylvania: they built homes, barns, and Presbyterian meetinghouses, tilled the land, pastured livestock, produced goods such as linen cloth, went to church, and reared their families. These new communities had considerable cultural meaning, though, for in settling them these families were forging a "Greater Pennsylvania" culture region that extended Scots Irish influence well beyond the state's borders, while simultaneously putting their unique stamp on southern backcountry and Appalachian culture.[23] And thanks to the choices they made and the communities they built, Pennsylvania's Scots Irish and their culture are thriving inside and outside the state.

NOTES

Introduction

1. Bernard Bailyn, *The Peopling of British North America: An Introduction* (New York: Vintage, 1988).

2. Kerby A. Miller, Arnold Schrier, Bruce D. Boling, and David N. Doyle, *Irish Immigrants in the Land of Canaan: Letters and Memoirs from Colonial and Revolutionary America, 1675–1815* (New York: Oxford University Press, 2003), 4.

3. For the "breed" notion, see Hubertis M. Cummings, *Scots Breed and Susquehanna* (Pittsburgh: University of Pittsburgh Press, 1964); for Andrew Jackson as a "born fighter," see Jim Webb, *Born Fighting: How the Scots-Irish Shaped America* (New York: Broadway Books, 2004), 19–20, 183–206, 288–291. See also Daniel W. Patterson, *The True Image: Gravestone Art and the Culture of Scotch Irish Settlers in the Pennsylvania and Carolina Backcountry* (Chapel Hill: University of North Carolina Press, 2012), 398–401.

4. See, for example, Charles K. Bolton, *Scotch Irish Pioneers in Ulster and America* (Baltimore: Genealogical Publishing, 1967); Cummings, *Scots Breed and Susquehanna;* Wayland F. Dunaway, *The Scotch-Irish of Colonial Pennsylvania* (Chapel Hill: University of North Carolina Press, 1944); James G. Leyburn, *The Scotch-Irish: A Social History* (Chapel Hill: University of North Carolina Press, 1962); Webb, *Born Fighting.*

5. Warren R. Hofstra, "From the North of Ireland to North America: The Scots-Irish and the Migration Experience," in *Ulster to America: The Scots-Irish Migration Experience, 1680–1830*, ed. Warren R. Hofstra (Knoxville: University of Tennessee Press, 2012), xiii.

6. J. D. Vance, *Hillbilly Elegy: A Memoir of Family and Culture in Crisis* (New York: HarperCollins, 2016). See also Alec MacGillis and Propublica, "The Original Underclass," *The Atlantic,* September 2016, https://www.theatlantic.com/magazine/archive/2016/09/the-original-underclass/492731/.

7. Patrick Griffin, *The People with No Name: Ireland's Ulster Scots, America's Scots Irish, and the Creation of a British Atlantic World, 1689–1764* (Princeton, NJ: Princeton University

Press, 2001), 2. See also Nancy Isenberg, *White Trash: The 400-Year Untold History of Class in America* (New York: Viking, 2016).

8. Griffin, *People with No Name*, 3; see also Patterson, *True Image*, 17–18.

9. David Noel Doyle, "Scots Irish or Scotch-Irish," in *Making the Irish American: History and Heritage of the Irish in the United States*, ed. J. J. Lee and Marion R. Casey (New York: New York University Press, 2006), 151–170; Griffin, *People with No Name*, 2, and 1–8; Miller et al., *Irish Immigrants*, 445–448; Michael Montgomery, "Scotch-Irish or Scots-Irish: What's in a Name?" *Tennessee Ancestors* 20 (2004): 143–150, http://www.ulsterscotslanguage. com/en/texts/scotch-irish/scotch-irish-or-scots-irish/. See also Patrick Griffin, "Searching for Independence: Revolutionary Kentucky, Irish American Experience, and Scotch-Irish Myth, 1770s–1790s," in Hofstra, *Ulster to America*, 221–225; Hofstra, "From the North of Ireland," xxv–xxvi; Judith Ridner, *A Town In-Between: Carlisle, Pennsylvania, and the Early Mid-Atlantic Interior* (Philadelphia: University of Pennsylvania Press, 2010), 103–104.

10. Miller et al., *Irish Immigrants*, 253, 261–267, 300.

11. No comprehensive study of the Scots Irish in early Pennsylvania has been written since Dunaway's well-known and oft-cited *Scotch-Irish of Colonial Pennsylvania* or the smaller and less-known work by James H. Smylie, *Scotch-Irish Presence in Pennsylvania* (University Park: Pennsylvania Historical Association, 1990).

Chapter 1

1. Alexander Crawford to Alexander Murray, quoted in Kerby A. Miller, Arnold Schrier, Bruce D. Boling, and David N. Doyle, *Irish Immigrants in the Land of Canaan: Letters and Memoirs from Colonial and Revolutionary America, 1675–1815* (New York: Oxford University Press, 2003), 25–26.

2. Henry Johnston to Moses Johnston, quoted in ibid., 32.

3. Ibid., 24–25, 30–31.

4. Audrey Horning, *Ireland in the Virginian Sea: Colonialism in the British Atlantic* (Chapel Hill: University of North Carolina Press, 2013), 19–25; James G. Leyburn, *The Scotch-Irish: A Social History* (Chapel Hill: University of North Carolina Press, 1962), 83; David W. Miller, "Searching for a New World: The Background and Baggage of Scots-Irish Immigrants," in *Ulster to America: The Scots-Irish Migration Experience, 1680–1830*, ed. Warren R. Hofstra (Knoxville: University of Tennessee Press, 2012), 4; Kerby A. Miller, *Emigrants and Exiles: Ireland and the Irish Exodus to North America* (New York: Oxford University Press, 1985), 15.

5. Quoted in Horning, *Ireland in the Virginian Sea*, 17.

6. Nicholas Canny, "The Marginal Kingdom: Ireland as a Problem in the First British Empire," in *Strangers within the Realm: Cultural Margins of the First British Empire*, ed. Bernard Bailyn and Philip D. Morgan (Chapel Hill: University of North Carolina Press, 1991), 37–39; Horning, *Ireland in the Virginian Sea*, 27. See also Miller, *Emigrants and Exiles*, 17–19.

7. Toby Barnard, *A New Anatomy of Ireland: The Irish Protestants, 1649–1770* (New Haven, CT: Yale University Press, 2003), 7.

8. Canny, "Marginal Kingdom," 37–43; Horning, *Ireland in the Virginian Sea*, 53–60; Leyburn, *Scotch-Irish*, 85–88; Miller, *Emigrants and Exiles*, 16–19.

9. Horning, *Ireland in the Virginian Sea*, 35 (quote); Barnard, *New Anatomy of Ireland*, 77.

10. Horning, *Ireland in the Virginian Sea*, 42–50, 60–67; Leyburn, *Scotch-Irish*, 85–87.

11. Horning, *Ireland in the Virginian Sea*, 93–99. For more about the Nine Years' War in Ireland, see Hiram Morgan, "Hugh O'Neill and the Nine Years War in Tudor England," *Historical Journal* 36, no.1 (1993): 21–37; James O'Neill, *The Nine Years War, 1593–1603: O'Neill, Mountjoy, and the Military Revolution* (Dublin: Four Courts Press, 2017).

12. Horning, *Ireland in the Virginian Sea*, 177–178. See also "Flight of the Earls," in *Wars and Conflict: The Plantation of Ulster*, BBC, accessed December 26, 2016, http://www.bbc.co.uk/history/british/plantation/planters/es02.shtml.

13. King James I to Sir Arthur Chichester, n.d., quoted in H. Tyler Blethen and Curtis W. Wood Jr., *From Ulster to Carolina: The Migration of the Scotch-Irish to Southwestern North Carolina* (Raleigh: North Carolina Department of Cultural Resources Office of Archives and History, 2005), 5. See also Horning, *Ireland in the Virginian Sea*, 53; Miller, "Searching for a New World," 4; Miller, *Emigrants and Exiles*, 19–20.

14. R. J. Dickson, *Ulster Immigration to Colonial America, 1718–1775* (Belfast: Ulster Historical Foundation, 1966), 2 (quote); Miller, *Emigrants and Exiles*, 20.

15. T. C. Smout, N. C. Landsman, and T. M. Devine, "Scottish Emigration in the Seventeenth and Eighteenth Centuries," in *Europeans on the Move: Studies on European Migration, 1500–1800*, ed. Nicholas Canny (Oxford, UK: Clarendon Press, 1994), 78–80, 85 (chart). Earlier estimates by Dickson put the number much higher, at one hundred thousand emigrants (*Ulster Immigration*, 3).

16. For more about the War of the Three Kingdoms, see Mark Stoyle, "Overview: Civil War and Revolution, 1603–1714," *History, British History*, BBC, accessed December 14, 2016, http://www.bbc.co.uk/history/british/civil_war_revolution/overview_civil_war_revolution_01.shtml.

17. For a general overview of Ireland's experience, see Micheál Ó Siochrú, "Ireland and the War of the Three Kingdoms," *History, British History*, BBC, accessed December 14, 2016, http://www.bbc.co.uk/history/british/civil_war_revolution/ireland_kingdoms_01.shtml; see also Horning, *Ireland in the Virginian Sea*, 262–266; Miller, *Emigrants and Exiles*, 20–21. For a more detailed examination of Ireland's 1641 Rising or Rebellion, see the essays in Brian Mac Cuarta, ed., *Ulster 1641: Aspects of the Rising* (Belfast: Institute for Irish Studies, 1997).

18. Miller, *Emigrants and Exiles*, 21. See also Louise Yeoman, "The Jacobite Cause," *History*, BBC, accessed December 15, 2016, http://www.bbc.co.uk/history/british/civil_war_revolution/scotland_jacobites_01.shtml; and *History, The Battle of the Boyne*, BBC, http://www.bbc.co.uk/history/events/battle_of_the_boyne. As Yeoman notes, members of Northern Ireland's Protestant Orange Order (named after William of Orange) still celebrate William's victory at the Battle of the Boyne every July 12.

19. Dickson, *Ulster Immigration*, 3; Patrick Griffin, *The People with No Name: Ireland's Ulster Scots, America's Scots Irish, and the Creation of a British Atlantic World, 1689–1764* (Princeton, NJ: Princeton University Press, 2001), 21; Miller, "Searching for a New World," 7–8; Vivienne Pollock, "The Household Economy in Early Rural America and Ulster: The Question of Self-Sufficiency," in *Ulster and North America: Transatlantic Perspectives on the Scotch-Irish*, ed. H. Tyler Blethen and Curtis W. Wood Jr. (Tuscaloosa: University of Alabama Press, 1997), 64; Smout, Landsman, and Devine, "Scottish Emigration," 87–88, 90; Robert Whan, *The Presbyterians of Ulster, 1680–1730* (Woodbridge, UK: Boydell Press, 2013), 5–6.

20. Raymond Gillespie, *Colonial Ulster: The Settlement of East Ulster, 1600–1641* (Cork: Cork University Press, 1985), 221 (quote); Philip Robinson, *The Plantation of Ulster* (Belfast: Ulster Historical Foundation, 1984), 192.

21. Gillespie, *Colonial Ulster*, 33; M. Perceval-Maxwell, *The Scottish Migration to Ulster in the Reign of James I* (London: Routledge and Kegan Paul, 1973), 94.

22. Gillespie, *Colonial Ulster*, 33–46; Perceval-Maxwell, *Scottish Migration to Ulster*, 33–45.

23. Smout, Landsman, and Devine, "Scottish Emigration," 78.

24. Pollock, "Household Economy," 63.

25. Blethen and Wood, *From Ulster to Carolina*, 5–6; Horning, *Ireland in the Virginian Sea*, 239; Pollock, "Household Economy," 64; Robinson, *Plantation of Ulster*, 129–135.

26. Canny, "Marginal Kingdom," 62; Gillespie, *Colonial Ulster*, 11 and chap. 4.

27. Canny, "Marginal Kingdom," 62–63; W. H. Crawford, *The Impact of the Domestic Linen Industry in Ulster* (Belfast: Ulster Historical Foundation, 2005), 87–88; Richard K. MacMaster, *Scotch-Irish Merchants in Colonial America* (Belfast: Ulster Historical Foundation, 2009), 11; Pollock, "Household Economy," 65–66.

28. Crawford, *Impact of the Domestic Linen Industry*, chap. 7 and 117; Harry Gribbon, "The Irish Linen Board, 1711–1828," in *The Warp of Ulster's Past*, ed. Marilyn Cohen (New York: St. Martin's Press, 1997), 71. Griffin, *People with No Name*, 25–30; MacMaster, *Scotch-Irish Merchants*, 9, 13–14. See also Jane Gray, *Spinning the Threads of Uneven Development: Gender and Industrialization in Ireland during the Long Eighteenth Century* (Oxford, UK: Lexington Books, 2005), chap. 2; N. B. Harte, "The British Linen Trade with the United States in the Eighteenth and Nineteenth Centuries," in *Textile Society of America Symposium Proceedings* (Lincoln: University of Nebraska, 1990), 15–16, 18–21, available at http://digitalcommons.unl.edu/tsaconf/605/.

29. Gribbon, "Irish Linen Board," 71–91; Griffin, *People with No Name*, 27–33. For women's role in the linen industry, see Crawford, *Impact of the Domestic Linen Industry*, chap. 9; Gray, *Spinning the Threads*, chap. 5, esp. 109–113.

30. Thomas M. Truxes, *Irish-American Trade, 1660–1783* (New York: Cambridge University Press, 1988), 35.

31. Griffin, *People with No Name*, 29–30.

32. Ibid., 32–35.

33. S. Scott Rohrer, *Wandering Souls: Protestant Migrations in America, 1630–1865* (Chapel Hill: University of North Carolina Press, 2010), 75–76.

34. Marilyn J. Westerkamp, *The Triumph of the Laity: Scots-Irish Piety and the Great Awakening, 1625–1760* (New York: Oxford University Press, 1988), 20–21. For more about Knox and the evolution of the Scottish Presbyterian Church (*Kirk*), see Rohrer, *Wandering Souls*, 86–92.

35. Whan, *Presbyterians of Ulster*, 178–182.

36. S. J. Connolly, "Ulster Presbyterians: Religion, Culture, and Politics, 1660–1850," in Blethen and Wood, *Ulster and North America*, 26–27, quote on 27.

37. Ibid., 28–29.

38. Westerkamp, *Triumph of the Laity*, 68–69.

39. Blethen and Wood, *From Ulster to Carolina*, 11–12, 14; Griffin, *People with No Name*, 19; Westerkamp, *Triumph of the Laity*, 69–70. See also Peter Brooke, *Ulster Presbyterianism: The Historical Perspective, 1610–1970* (New York: St. Martin's Press, 1987), 59–62.

40. Whan, *Presbyterians of Ulster*, 13.

41. Westerkamp, *Triumph of the Laity*, 69.

42. Whan, *Presbyterians of Ulster*, 3–4, 8–9, 59–60, 62. See also Brooke, *Ulster Presbyterianism*, 67–72; Wayland F. Dunaway, *The Scotch-Irish of Colonial Pennsylvania* (Chapel Hill: University of North Carolina Press, 1944), 31. The Test Act was not repealed until 1780.

43. Dickson, *Ulster Immigration* 10–14; Dunaway, *Scotch-Irish of Colonial Pennsylvania*, 29–30.

44. Johnston to Johnston, quoted in Miller et al., *Irish Immigrants*, 32; Dickson, *Ulster Immigration* 9–13; Whan, *Presbyterians of Ulster*, 9.

Chapter 2

1. James Magraw to John Magraw, May 21, 1733, quoted in Kerby A. Miller, Arnold Schrier, Bruce D. Boling, and David N. Doyle, *Irish Immigrants in the Land of Canaan: Letters and Memoirs from Colonial and Revolutionary America, 1675–1815* (New York: Oxford University Press, 2003), 145.

2. For more about James Logan and his efforts to settle Ulster immigrants in south-central Pennsylvania, see Patrick Spero, *Frontier Country: The Politics of War in Early Pennsylvania* (Philadelphia: University of Pennsylvania Press, 2016), 39–42.

3. Miller et al., *Irish Immigrants*, 143–144; Belle McKinney Hays Swope, *History of Middle Spring Presbyterian Church, Middle Spring, Pa. 1738–1900* (Newville, PA: Times Steam Printing House, 1900), 5–8. For the risks in settling Pennsylvania's west during the 1730s, see Spero, *Frontier Country*, chap. 4. David Noel Doyle, "Scots Irish or Scotch-Irish," in *Making the Irish American: History and Heritage of the Irish in the United States*, ed. J. J. Lee and Marion R. Casey (New York: New York University Press, 2006), challenges the popular belief that these Scots Irish colonists chose life on the frontier, observing: "The newcomers to American did *not* choose the wilderness as such" (164).

4. Sally Schwartz, *"A Mixed Multitude": The Struggle for Toleration in Colonial Pennsylvania* (New York: New York University Press, 1987), 15 (quote) and chap. 2. For the history of the founding of Pennsylvania, see also Susan Klepp, "Encounter and Experiment: The Colonial Period," in *Pennsylvania: A History of the Commonwealth*, ed. Randall M. Miller and William Pencak (University Park: Pennsylvania State University Press, 2002), 61–69.

5. William Penn quoted in Schwartz, *"Mixed Multitude,"* 15.

6. Alan Taylor, *American Colonies* (New York: Penguin, 2001), 265–267. For the Irish grid plan connection, see Gilbert Camblin, *The Town in Ulster* (Belfast: William Mullan and Son, 1951), chap. 3.

7. Schwartz, *"Mixed Multitude,"* 23; Marilyn J. Westerkamp, *The Triumph of the Laity: Scots-Irish Piety and the Great Awakening, 1625–1760* (New York: Oxford University Press, 1988, 136.

8. Klepp, "Encounter and Experiment," 61 (chart).

9. Taylor, *American Colonies*, 267 (quote), 269; Schwartz, *"Mixed Multitude,"* 36.

10. U.S. Bureau of the Census, "Population in the Colonial and Continental Periods," in *A Century of Population Growth: From the First Census of the United States to the Twelfth, 1790–1900* (Washington, D.C.: Government Printing Office, 1909), https://www2.census .gov/prod2/decennial/documents/00165897ch01.pdf; Lawrence Yun, "Largest Cities in the United States in 1776 and in 2076," *Economists' Outlook* (blog), July 3, 2012, http://econo

mistsoutlook.blogs.realtor.org/2012/07/03/largest-cities-in-the-united-states-in-1776-and-in-2076/.

11. Redemptioners, like indentured servants, were immigrants who were unable to pay the cost of their ship passage to America. Unlike indentured servants, however, who typically signed a labor contract specifying their term of service (indenture) before embarking on their voyage, redemptioners sailed without either an indenture or paid passage. Once they arrived in America, they had a short period in which to "redeem" themselves by finding a relative or friend to pay the cost of their passage. If that happened, they went free. If it did not, the ship's captain had the right to sell the redemptioner as a servant to the highest bidder in order to repay the cost of Atlantic transport. For more on redemptioners, see Karl Frederick Geiser, *Redemptioner and Indentured Servants in the Colony and Commonwealth of Pennsylvania*, supplement, *Yale Review*, 10, no. 2 (August 1901): 6–7, https://archive.org/stream/redemptionersind00geis/redemptionersind00geis_djvu.txt.

12. James T. Lemon, *The Best Poor Man's Country: A Geographical Study of Early Southeastern Pennsylvania* (New York: W. W. Norton, 1972); R. J. Dickson, *Ulster Emigration to Colonial America, 1718–1775* (Belfast: Ulster Historical Foundation, 1966), 224.

13. Doyle, "Scots Irish or Scotch Irish," 151. Miller et al., *Irish Immigrants*, 4, estimates the total number of eighteenth-century Irish emigrants at four hundred thousand, noting, however, that though this number seems small compared with the massive number of Catholic Irish who departed during the nineteenth century, it represents a substantial exodus within Ulster's Scots Irish community, which, in the 1750s, stood at less than five hundred thousand.

14. Patrick Griffin, *The People with No Name: Ireland's Ulster Scots, America's Scots Irish, and the Creation of a British Atlantic World, 1689–1764* (Princeton, NJ: Princeton University Press, 2001), 1.

15. Benjamin Bankhurst, *Ulster Presbyterians and the Scots-Irish Diaspora, 1750–1764* (London: Palgrave Macmillan, 2013), 13; Dickson, *Ulster Emigration*, 221–222, 226; Richard K. MacMaster, *Scotch-Irish Merchants in Colonial America* (Belfast: Ulster Historical Foundation, 2009), 3–4, Griffin, *People with No Name*, 90–91.

16. Dickson, *Ulster Emigration*, 225 (chart).

17. Marianne S. Wokeck, *Trade in Strangers: The Beginnings of Mass Migration to North America* (University Park: Pennsylvania State University Press, 1999), 172–173 (chart).

18. Bankhurst, *Ulster Presbyterians*, 13.

19. Ibid., 13–14; Griffin, *People with No Name*, 67–73.

20. Wokeck, *Trade in Strangers*, 169–171.

21. James Logan quoted in Maldwyn Jones, "The Scotch-Irish in British America," in *Strangers within the Realm: Cultural Margins of the First British Empire*, ed. Bernard Bailyn and Philip D. Morgan (Chapel Hill: University of North Carolina Press, 1991), 297; see also Schwartz, *"Mixed Multitude,"* 85–87.

22. Wokeck, *Trade in Strangers*, 175; see also Bankhurst, *Ulster Presbyterians*, 18; Thomas M. Truxes, *Irish-American Trade, 1660–1783* (New York: Cambridge University Press, 1988), 129.

23. For more on the Hearts of Steel or Steelboys movement, see Tony Canavan, "Illoyal, Lawless, Irreligious Banditti: The Hearts of Steel—An Ulster Insurrection," *History Ireland* 7, no. 4 (July 1999): 22–26.

24. Dickson, *Ulster Emigration*, 69–77.

25. Wokeck, *Trade in Strangers*, 175.

26. U.S. Bureau of the Census, "Population in the Colonial and Continental Periods."

27. Wokeck, *Trade in Strangers*, 177.

28. David Noel Doyle, *Ireland, Irishmen, and Revolutionary America, 1760–1820* (Dublin: Mercier Press, 1981), 42; Griffin, *People with No Name*, 92; MacMaster, *Scotch-Irish Merchants*, 69; Truxes, *Irish-American Trade*, chap. 10. As MacMaster notes, the flaxseed trade between Ireland and the American colonies was an eighteenth-century phenomenon that arose after the British Board of Trade opened Irish ports to colonial American produce in 1731 (*Scotch-Irish Merchants*, 16–17).

29. MacMaster, *Scotch-Irish Merchants*, 47–57; Wokeck, *Trade in Strangers*, 198; see also Truxes, *Irish-American Trade*, chaps. 7 and 9.

30. Bankhurst, *Ulster Presbyterians*, 19.

31. Irish wage rates are difficult to obtain, but for a general discussion of English wages of the time see "Currency, Coinage, and the Cost of Living," *The Proceedings of the Old Bailey, London's Central Criminal Court, 1674 to 1913*, accessed January 23, 2017, https://www.oldbaileyonline.org/static/Coinage.jsp#reading-costofliving.

32. Wokeck, *Trade in Strangers*, 198–208; Miller et al., *Irish Immigrants*, 90. For a first-person account of a journey gone bad, see the 1762 account of County Down emigrant John Smylie, in Miller et al., *Irish Immigrants*, 91–93.

33. Griffin, *People with No Name*, 93.

34. *Pennsylvania Gazette*, February 26, 1751, 2, America's Historical Newspapers, Readex, available at http://www.readex.com/content/americas-historical-newspapers.

35. Wokeck, *Trade in Strangers*, 187.

36. Bernard Bailyn, *Voyagers to the West: A Passage in the Peopling of America on the Eve of Revolution* (New York: Vintage Books, 1988), 166.

37. For German comparison, see Wokeck, *Trade in Strangers*, 48–52.

38. Wokeck, *Trade in Strangers*, 186.

39. Doyle, "Scots-Irish or Scotch Irish," 163.

40. Miller et al., *Irish Immigrants*, 143–146.

41. Magraw to Magraw quoted in Miller et al., *Irish Immigrants*, 145.

42. Wayland F. Dunaway, *The Scotch-Irish of Colonial Pennsylvania* (Chapel Hill: University of North Carolina Press, 1944), 59.

43. Spero, *Frontier Country*, 128.

44. Craig W. Horle, "William West," in *Lawmaking and Legislators in Pennsylvania: A Biographical Dictionary*, vol. 2, *1710–1756*, ed. Joseph F. Foster, David Haugaard, Craig W. Horle, Carolyn M. Peters, Jeffrey L. Scheib, and Laurie M. Wolfe (Philadelphia: University of Pennsylvania Press, 1997), 1055–1064; Judith Ridner, *A Town In-Between: Carlisle, Pennsylvania, and the Early Mid-Atlantic Interior* (Philadelphia: University of Pennsylvania Press, 2010), 52; Spero, *Frontier Country*, 128–129, 136–137; Truxes, *Irish-American Trade*, 141; Pennsylvania Historical and Museum Commission, Hope Lodge, "History of Hope Lodge," accessed February 10, 2018, http://www.historichopelodge.org/history/; Paul A. W. Wallace, "Historic Hope Lodge," *Pennsylvania Magazine of History and Biography* 86, no. 2 (April 1962): 115–142.

45. As Ned Landsman notes in *Crossroads of Empire: The Middle Colonies in British North America* (Baltimore: Johns Hopkins University Press, 2010), "[not] all Ulster Protestants descended from Scots: there was substantial English Protestant settlement in Ulster

also, although the two groups concentrated their settlements in different parts of northern Ireland" (129).

46. William Irvine quoted in Judith Ridner, "William Irvine and the Complexities of Manhood and Fatherhood in the Pennsylvania Backcountry," *Pennsylvania Magazine of History and Biography* 125, nos. 1 and 2 (January/April 2001), 14; see also 5–34; Ridner, *Town In-Between*, 118–120, 192–193. See also "Dr. William Irvine," Irvineclan.com, accessed January 25, 2017, http://www.irvineclan.com/wi1741.htm.

Chapter 3

1. James McCullough, "James McCullough Journal, 1748–1758," quoted in *Irish Immigrants in the Land of Canaan: Letters and Memoirs from Colonial and Revolutionary America, 1675–1815*, ed. Kerby A. Miller, Arnold Schrier, Bruce D. Boling, and David N. Doyle (New York: Oxford University Press, 2003), 160–163.

2. Sally Schwartz, *"A Mixed Multitude": The Struggle for Toleration in Colonial Pennsylvania* (New York: New York University Press, 1987), chap. 1.

3. Maldwyn Jones, "The Scotch-Irish in British America," in *Strangers within the Realm: Cultural Margins of the First British Empire*, ed. Bernard Bailyn and Philip D. Morgan (Chapel Hill: University of North Carolina Press, 1991), 297–298.

4. Thomas L. Purvis, "Patterns of Ethnic Settlement in Late Eighteenth-Century Pennsylvania," *Western Pennsylvania Historical Magazine* 70, no. 2 (April 1987): 117. See also "Nationality Groups in Pennsylvania in 1790, as a Percentage of Population" (chart), in *Pennsylvania: A History of the Commonwealth*, ed. Randall M. Miller and William Pencak (University Park: Pennsylvania State University Press, 2002), 135.

5. D. G. Hart, *Calvinism: A History* (New Haven, CT: Yale University Press, 2013), 122.

6. Thomas M. Truxes, *Irish-American Trade, 1660–1783* (New York: Cambridge University Press, 1988), 40–144.

7. Sharon V. Salinger, "Colonial Labor in Transition: The Decline of Indentured Servitude in Late Eighteenth-Century Philadelphia," *Labor History* 22, no. 2 (Spring 1981): 165–180; Salinger, *"To Serve Well and Faithfully": Labor and Indentured Servants in Pennsylvania, 1682–1800* (New York: Cambridge University Press, 1987), 134–136; Billy G. Smith, *The "Lower Sort": Philadelphia's Laboring People, 1750–1800* (Ithaca, NY: Cornell University Press, 1990), chaps. 5 and 7.

8. David Noel Doyle, *Ireland, Irishmen and Revolutionary America, 1760–1820* (Dublin: Mercer Press, 1981), 89–90; "William Allen," in *Lawmaking and Legislators in Pennsylvania: A Biographical Dictionary*, vol. 3, *1757–1775*, ed. Craig W. Horle, Joseph S. Foster, and Laurie M. Wolfe (Harrisburg: House of Representatives, Commonwealth of Pennsylvania, 2005), 231–280; Bradley Maule, "Following Allens/Allen's/Allen Land to the Origins of Mount Airy," Hidden City Philadelphia, accessed January 20, 2017, http://hiddencityphila .org/2014/01/following-allensallensallen-lane-to-the-origins-of-mount-airy/.

9. Doyle, *Ireland, Irishmen*, 90.

10. Judith Ridner, *A Town In-Between: Carlisle, Pennsylvania, and the Early Mid-Atlantic Interior* (Philadelphia: University of Pennsylvania Press, 2010), 55. See also Merri Lou Schaumann, *Cumberland County, Pennsylvania Taverns, 1750–1840* (Lewisbury: W and M Printing, for the Cumberland County Historical Society, 1994), 56.

11. Ridner, *Town In-Between*, 51–56, 80, 97–103. See also Patrick Griffin, *The People with*

No Name: Ireland's Ulster Scots, America's Scots Irish, and the Creation of a British Atlantic World, 1689–1764 (Princeton, NJ: Princeton University Press, 2001), 111–112; Richard K. MacMaster, *Scotch-Irish Merchants in Colonial America* (Belfast: Ulster Historical Foundation, 2009), 111–117.

12. Warren R. Hofstra, *The Planting of New Virginia: Settlement and Landscape in the Shenandoah Valley* (Baltimore: Johns Hopkins University Press, 2004), chap. 3.

13. David L. Preston, *The Texture of Contact: European and Indian Settler Communities on the Frontiers of Iroquoia, 1667–1783* (Lincoln: University of Nebraska Press, 2009), chap. 3. See also Griffin, *People with No Name*, chap. 4.

14. E. Estyn Evans, "The Scotch-Irish: Their Cultural Adaptation and Heritage in the American Old West," in *Essays in Scotch-Irish History*, ed. E. R. R. Green (New York: Routledge and Kegan Paul, 1969), 76–79; Jones, "Scotch-Irish in British America," 295–298; Preston, *Texture of Contact*, 155–158.

15. David Hackett Fischer, *Albion's Seed: Four British Folkways in America* (New York: Oxford University Press, 1989), 655–662; John B. Rehder, "The Scotch-Irish and English in Appalachia," in *To Build a New Land: Ethnic Landscapes in North America*, ed. Allen G. Noble (Baltimore: Johns Hopkins University Press, 1992), 103–104. See also Evans, "Scotch-Irish," 78–80; Doyle, *Ireland, Irishmen*, 82–83; Jones, "Scotch-Irish in British America," 306.

16. Jones, "Scotch-Irish in British America," 298–299; Evans, "Scotch-Irish," 80–84.

17. Adrienne Hood, "The Material World of Cloth: Production and Use in Eighteenth-Century Rural Pennsylvania," *William and Mary Quarterly*, 3d. ser., 53, no. 1 (January 1996): 53.

18. Griffin, *People with No Name*, 105–113, quote on 109. See also H. Tyler Blethen and Curtis W. Wood Jr., *From Ulster to Carolina: The Migration of the Scotch-Irish to Southwestern North Carolina* (Raleigh: North Carolina Department of Cultural Resources Office of Archives and History, 2005), 31; Doyle, *Ireland, Irishmen*, 87–88; Jones, "Scotch-Irish in British America," 298–301. For the best study of flax and linen production in rural Pennsylvania, see Adrienne Hood, *The Weaver's Craft: Cloth, Commerce, and Industry in Early Pennsylvania* (Philadelphia: University of Pennsylvania Press, 2003).

19. Griffin, *People with No Name*, 103; Jones, "Scotch-Irish in British America," 300; Schwartz, *"Mixed Multitude,"* 200–202.

20. James T. Lemon, "The Agricultural Practices of National Groups in Eighteenth-Century Southeastern Pennsylvania," *Geographical Review* 56, no. 4 (October 1966): 467–496. See also Jones, "Scotch-Irish in British America," 300–302.

21. Blethen and Wood, *From Ulster to Carolina*, 30–31.

22. Michael B. Montgomery, "The Scotch-Irish Element in Appalachian English: How Broad? How Deep?" in Blethen and Wood, *Ulster and North America*, 189–212.

23. Wendy A. Cooper and Lisa Minardi, *Paint, Pattern, and People: Furniture of Southeastern Pennsylvania* (Philadelphia: University of Pennsylvania Press, 2011), 21–26; for the Germans, see 26–59. For German houses, see Bernard L. Herman, *Town House: Architecture and Material Life in the Early American City* (Chapel Hill: University of North Carolina Press, 2005), 85–88.

24. Daniel W. Patterson, *The True Image: Gravestone Art and the Culture of Scotch Irish Settlers in the Pennsylvania and Carolina Backcountry* (Chapel Hill: University of North Carolina Press, 2012), 21–29.

25. Jones, "Scotch-Irish in British America," 302.

26. Randall Balmer and John R. Fitzmier, *The Presbyterians* (Westport, CT: Praeger, 1994), 15; Elizabeth I. Nybakken, "New Light on the Old Side: Irish Influences on Colonial Presbyterianism," *Journal of American History* 68, no. 4 (March 1982): 817–819.

27. James G. Leyburn, *The Scotch-Irish: A Social History* (Chapel Hill: University of North Carolina Press, 1962), 273. See also Ned C. Landsman, *Scotland and Its First American Colony, 1683–1765* (Princeton, NJ: Princeton University Press, 1985).

28. Balmer and Fitzmier, *Presbyterians*, 24.

29. Ibid., 25; Wayland F. Dunaway, *The Scotch-Irish of Colonial Pennsylvania* (Chapel Hill: University of North Carolina Press, 1944), 203; Hart, *Calvinism*, 123–124; Jones, "Scotch-Irish in British America," 302; Marilyn J. Westerkamp, *The Triumph of the Laity: Scots-Irish Piety and the Great Awakening, 1625–1760* (New York: Oxford University Press, 1988, 143–144.

30. Peter Brooke, *Ulster Presbyterianism: The Historical Perspective, 1610–1970* (New York: St. Martin's Press, 1987), chap. 4; Balmer and Fitzmier, *Presbyterians*, chap. 2; Nybakken, "New Light on Old Side," 819–820; Griffin, *People with No Name*, 114–115.

31. Dunaway, *Scotch-Irish of Colonial Pennsylvania*, 204; Griffin, *People with No Name*, 116.

32. Dunaway, *Scotch-Irish of Colonial Pennsylvania*, 207–208; Griffin, *People with No Name*, 114; Leyburn, *Scotch-Irish*, 274–276.

33. Griffin, *People with No Name*, 114.

34. Ibid., 117; Westerkamp, *Triumph of the Laity*, chap. 6.

35. Thomas S. Kidd, *The Great Awakening: The Roots of Evangelical Christianity in Colonial America* (New Haven, CT: Yale University Press, 2007), xviii.

36. Balmer and Fitzmier, *Presbyterians*, 27; Leyburn, *Scotch-Irish*, 277; Westerkamp, *Triumph of the Laity*, 155, 167–168.

37. Balmer and Fitzmier, *Presbyterians*, 27–30.

38. Leyburn, *Scotch-Irish*, 280–281; Westerkamp, *Triumph of the Laity*, 172–176.

39. Kidd, *Great Awakening*, 45–50; Westerkamp, *Triumph of the Laity*, 187.

40. Francis Alison quoted in Nybakken, "New Light on Old Side," 824; see also 822–823.

41. Ibid., 824–825; Griffin, *People with No Name*, 154–155; Wilfred Earnest Tabb, "The Presbyterian Clergy of the Great Awakening" (PhD diss., Washington University, 1992), 215–234.

42. Rev. George Duffield quoted in Ridner, *Town In-Between*, 61.

43. Ibid., 60–61; Richard Tritt, "The Rocky Road to the Meeting House," First Presbyterian Church of Carlisle, accessed May 15, 2017, http://www.firstprescarlisle.org/our-history/the-rocky-road-to-the-meeting-house/.

Chapter 4

1. Benjamin Franklin, *A Narrative of the Late Massacres, in Lancaster County, of a Number of Indians, Friends of this Province, By Persons Unknown. With some Observations on the same* (Philadelphia, 1764), 8, 9.

2. The following works are the most recent and most relevant in the voluminous literature on the Paxton Boys: Benjamin Bankhurst, "A Looking-Glass for Presbyterians:

Recasting Prejudice in Late Colonial Pennsylvania," *Pennsylvania Magazine of History and Biography* 133, no. 4 (October 2009): 317–348; Jack Brubaker, *Massacre of the Conestogas: On the Trail of the Paxton Boys in Lancaster County* (Charleston, SC: History Press, 2010); Krista Camenzind, "Violence, Race, and the Paxton Boys," in *Friends and Enemies in Penn's Woods*, ed. William Pencak and Daniel Richter (University Park: Pennsylvania State University Press, 2004): 201–220; Jeremy Engels, "'Equipped for Murder': The Paxton Boys and 'the Spirit of Killing All Indians' in Pennsylvania, 1763–1764," *Rhetoric and Public Affairs* 8, no. 3 (2005): 355–382; Patrick Griffin, *American Leviathan* (New York: Hill and Wang, 2007); Kevin Kenny, *Peaceable Kingdom Lost: The Paxton Boys and the Destruction of William Penn's Holy Experiment* (New York: Oxford University Press, 2009); Alison Olson, "The Pamphlet War over the Paxton Boys," *Pennsylvania Magazine of History and Biography* 123, nos. 1 and 2 (January–April 1999): 31–55; Peter Silver, *Our Savage Neighbors: How Indian War Transformed Early America* (New York: W. W. Norton, 2008); Patrick Spero, *Frontier Country: The Politics of War in Early Pennsylvania* (Philadelphia: University of Pennsylvania Press, 2016). See also the collection of essays that appeared in the Spring 2016 issue of *Early American Studies*.

3. Franklin, *Narrative of the Late Massacres*, 27.

4. Olson, "Pamphlet War," 31–55. For the emotional language of this debate, see Nicole Eustace, *Passion Is the Gale: Emotion, Power, and the Coming of the American Revolution* (Chapel Hill: University of North Carolina Press, 2008), chap. 8.

5. Many recent works challenge us to reconsider notions of Pennsylvania as an idealized "peaceable kingdom" by detailing the history of building cultural tensions before 1750. Among the most important are James H. Merrell, *Into the American Woods: Negotiators on the Pennsylvania Frontier* (New York: Norton, 2000); Jane T. Merritt, *At the Crossroads: Indians and Empires on a Mid-Atlantic Frontier, 1700–1763* (Chapel Hill: University of North Carolina Press, 2003); David L. Preston, *The Texture of Contact: European and Indian Settler Communities on the Frontiers of Iroquoia, 1667–1783* (Lincoln: University of Nebraska Press, 2009); Silver, *Our Savage Neighbors*; Spero, *Frontier Country*.

6. For Pennsylvania politics at mid-century, see James Hutson, *Pennsylvania Politics, 1746–1770* (Princeton, NJ: Princeton University Press, 1972); Alan Tully, *Forming American Politics: Ideals, Interests, and Institutions in Colonial New York and Pennsylvania* (Baltimore: Johns Hopkins University Press, 1994); and Tully, *William Penn's Legacy: Politics and Social Structure in Provincial Pennsylvania, 1726–1755* (Baltimore: Johns Hopkins University Press, 1977). For the Conojocular War, see Spero, *Frontier Country*, chap. 4.

7. Richard Peters quoted in Judith Ridner, *A Town In-Between: Carlisle, Pennsylvania, and the Early Mid-Atlantic Interior* (Philadelphia: University of Pennsylvania Press, 2010), 47.

8. Samuel Hazard, ed., *Minutes of the Provincial Council of Pennsylvania, from the Organization to the Termination of the Proprietary Government*, 10 vols. (Philadelphia: Joseph Severns, 1851–1852), 5:443, quoted in Ridner, *Town In-Between*, 47.

9. Spero, *Frontier Country*, 94, 95. This overview is drawn in large part from Kenny, *Peaceable Kingdom Lost*, chaps. 2–5. For Indian perspectives, see Daniel K. Richter, *Facing East from Indian Country: A Native History of Early America* (Cambridge, MA: Harvard University Press, 2001), chap. 5.

10. Matthew C. Ward, *Breaking the Backcountry: The Seven Years' War in Virginia and Pennsylvania, 1754–1765* (Pittsburgh: University of Pittsburgh Press, 2003), chaps. 1 and 2; Kenny, *Peaceable Kingdom Lost*, chap. 6

11. Ward, *Breaking the Backcountry*, 67; see also chap. 3.

12. Kenny, *Peaceable Kingdom Lost*, 71.

13. Hubertis M. Cummings, *Scots-Breed and Susquehanna* (Pittsburgh: University of Pittsburgh Press, 1964), 72; Silver, *Our Savage Neighbors*, 67.

14. *Pennsylvania Gazette*, April 8, 1756, and Col. Henry Bouquet quoted in Ridner, *Town In-Between*, 82. For the devastation, see Daniel Barr, "Victory at Kittanning? Reevaluating the Impact of Armstrong's Raid on the Seven Years' War in Pennsylvania," *Pennsylvania Magazine of History and Biography* 131, no. 1 (January 2007): 13–14.

15. Ridner, *Town In-Between*, 83; see also Barr, "Victory at Kittanning?," 14–18.

16. Ward, *Breaking the Backcountry*, 66.

17. Kenny, *Peaceable Kingdom Lost*, 76; Cummings, *Scots-Breed and Susquehanna*, 76–77.

18. Ward, *Breaking the Backcountry*, 106; Barr, "Victory at Kittanning?," 18–19.

19. Barr, "Victory at Kittanning?," 10–11, 18–19.

20. Ibid., 27; Kenny, *Peaceable Kingdom Lost*, 88–89; Ridner, *Town In-Between*, 85–87.

21. Barr, "Victory at Kittanning?," 19–21.

22. Ibid., 21–22, 29; Ward, *Breaking the Backcountry*, 106–107.

23. Ridner, *Town In-Between*, 87; "Kittanning Historical Marker," ExplorePAhistory. com, http://explorepahistory.com/hmarker.php?markerId=1-A-220.

24. Ridner, *Town In-Between*, 89; Ward, *Breaking the Backcountry*, 70–90.

25. Kenny, *Peaceable Kingdom Lost*, 117–118.

26. John Elder to Gov. James Hamilton, August 4, 1763, Elder Collection, Historical Society of Dauphin County, Harrisburg, PA.

27. Kenny, *Peaceable Kingdom Lost*, 119–121.

28. Ibid., 123–125. For "anti-Indian sublime," see Silver, *Our Savage Neighbors*, 83–94, chap. 5. For Indian hating, see Richard White, *The Middle Ground: Indians, Empires, and Republics in the Great Lakes Region, 1650–1815* (Cambridge: Cambridge University Press, 1992), chap. 9.

29. Matthew Smith and James Gibson, *A Declaration and Remonstrance Of the distressed and bleeding Frontier Inhabitants of the Province of Pennsylvania, . . .* (Philadelphia, 1764), 8; Philopatrius [David James Dove], *The Quaker Unmask'd; or, Plain Truth: Humbly address'd to the Consideration of all the Freemen of Pennsylvania* (Philadelphia, 1764), 5. For a general discussion of ethno-religious tensions in the colony at this time, see Silver, *Our Savage Neighbors*.

30. Kenny, *Peaceable Kingdom Lost*, 125–129.

31. Griffin, *American Leviathan*, 46–47. For local dynamics in Lancaster, see Scott Paul Gordon, "The Paxton Boys and Edward Shippen: Defiance and Deference on a Collapsing Frontier," *Early American Studies* (Spring 2016): 319–347.

32. Elder to Hamilton, September 13, 1763, Elder Collection.

33. Matthäus Hehl quoted in Gordon, "Paxton Boys and Edward Shippen," 329.

34. Engels, "'Equipped for Murder,'" 356; see also Brubaker, *Massacre of the Conestogas*, pt. 1; Kenny, *Peaceable Kingdom Lost*, 134–136,

35. Engels, "'Equipped for Murder,'" 355.

36. Kenny, *Peaceable Kingdom Lost*, 140–142.

37. Hehl quoted in Gordon, "Paxton Boys and Edward Shippen," 330.

38. Kenny, *Peaceable Kingdom Lost*, 147–148.

39. Ibid., 162–163.

40. Matthew Smith and James Gibson, *Declaration and Remonstrance*, 3–4.

41. Ibid., 10–18.

42. Kenny, *Peaceable Kingdom Lost*, 163–168.

43. Olson, "Pamphlet War," 31. See also Eustace, *Passion Is the Gale*, chap. 8; Silver, *Our Savage Neighbors*, chap. 7. For a digitized archive of these pamphlets, see Will Fenton, "Digital Paxton," http://digitalpaxton.org.

44. Franklin, *Narrative*, 7, 13, 26–27. For Franklin's hatred of Presbyterians and his anti-Irish prejudice, see Benjamin Bankhurst, "Early Irish America and Its Enemies: Ethnic Identity Formation in the Era of the American Revolution, 1760–1820," *Journal of Irish and Scottish Studies* 5, no. 2 (Spring 2012): 17–38; Kenny, *Peaceable Kingdom Lost*, 173–174. For unbridled emotion and its connection to civility and masculinity, see Eustace, *Passion Is the Gale*, chap. 8.

45. Bankhurst, "Looking-Glass for Presbyterians," 324–325.

46. Silver, *Our Savage Neighbors*, 204.

47. *A Touch of the Times. A New Song. To the Tune of Nancy Dawson* (Philadelphia, 1764), 3.

48. Isaac Hunt, *A Letter From a Gentleman in Transilvania to his Friend in America*, (Philadelphia, 1764), 4, Digital Paxton, http://digitalpaxton.org/works/digital-paxton/a-let ter-from-a-gentleman-in-transilvania-to-his-friend-in-america?path=a-touch-on-the-times; Bankhurst, "Looking-Glass for Presbyterians," 340, 330–334.

49. Philopatrius, *Quaker Unmask'd*, 5.

50. Olson, "Pamphlet War," 44–46; Silver, *Our Savage Neighbors*, chap. 7.

51. Eustace, *Passion Is the Gale*, chap. 8; Eustace, "The Sentimental Paradox: Humanity and Violence on the Pennsylvania Frontier," *William and Mary Quarterly*, 3d. ser., 65, no. 1 (January 2008): 29–64; Kenny, *Peaceable Kingdom Lost*, 201–202.

52. Spero, *Frontier Country*, 170–187.

53. Kenny, *Peaceable Kingdom Lost*, 205–206.

Chapter 5

1. Job Johnson, Philadelphia, to Robert Johnson, Slaghtybogy, Maghera Parish, County Londonderry, Ireland, December 5, 1784, quoted in Kerby A. Miller, Arnold Schrier, Bruce D. Boling, and David N. Doyle, *Irish Immigrants in the Land of Canaan: Letters and Memoirs from Colonial and Revolutionary America, 1675–1815* (New York: Oxford University Press, 2003), 569.

2. Ibid. 567–571.

3. Ibid, 515. See also Benjamin Bankhurst, "Early Irish America and its Enemies: Ethnic Identity Formation in the Era of the American Revolution, 1760–1820," *Journal of Irish and Scottish Studies* 5, no. 2 (Spring 2012): 27–28.

4. John Dickinson quoted in William Pencak, "The Promise of Revolution, 1750–1800," in *Pennsylvania: A History of the Commonwealth*, ed. Randall M. Miller and William Pencak (University Park: Pennsylvania State University Press, 2002), 116.

5. Richard Alan Ryerson, *The Revolution Is Now Begun: The Radical Committees of Philadelphia, 1765–1776* (Philadelphia: University of Pennsylvania Press, 1978), 19; David Noel Doyle, *Ireland, Irishmen, and Revolutionary America, 1760–1820* (Dublin: Mercier Press, 1981), 123; Joseph Foster, *In Pursuit of Equal Liberty: George Bryan and the Revolution in Pennsylvania* (University Park: Pennsylvania State University Press, 1994), 67.

6. Doyle, *Ireland, Irishmen*, 123–124.

7. Ibid., 113; see also 90, 113–117, 124; Miller et al., *Irish Immigrants*, 476–484, 520–521n42.

8. Doyle, *Ireland, Irishmen*, 114. For more on Alison, see "Francis Alison (1705–1779)," Penn Biographies, accessed May 21, 2017, http://www.archives.upenn.edu/people/1700s/alison_fra.html.

9. Pencak, "Promise of Revolution," 116, 118.

10. Patrick Spero, *Frontier Country: The Politics of War in Early Pennsylvania* (Philadelphia: University of Pennsylvania Press, 2016), 223–227, quote on 227; Pencak, "Promise of Revolution," 118.

11. Robert G. Crist, "Cumberland County," in *Beyond Philadelphia: The American Revolution in the Pennsylvania Hinterland*, ed. John B. Frantz and William Pencak (University Park: Pennsylvania State University Press, 1998), 118–120.

12. Francis Alison quoted in Maurice J. Bric, *Ireland, Philadelphia, and the Re-Inventions of America, 1760–1800* (Dublin: Four Courts Press, 2008), 60.

13. Doyle, *Ireland, Irishmen*, 126–128; Pencak, "Promise of Revolution," 121, 123, 126; Spero, *Frontier Country*, 223–233. See also Owen S. Ireland, *Religion, Ethnicity, and Politics: Ratifying the Constitution in Pennsylvania* (University Park: Pennsylvania State University Press, 1995), 11.

14. Owen S. Ireland, "The Crux of Politics: Religion and Party in Pennsylvania, 1778–1789," *William and Mary Quarterly*, 3d. ser., 42, no. 4 (Oct. 1985): 454–455.

15. Ireland, "Crux of Politics," 455; Doyle, *Ireland, Irishmen*, 130.

16. Miller et al., *Irish Immigrants*, 567.

17. Crist, "Cumberland County," 122–124.

18. Judith Ridner, *A Town In-Between: Carlisle, Pennsylvania, and the Early Mid-Atlantic Interior* (Philadelphia: University of Pennsylvania Press, 2010), 122; Crist, "Cumberland County," 124–126.

19. Crist, "Cumberland County," 126.

20. Ridner, *Town In-Between*, 122–123. See also Gregory Knouff, *The Soldiers' Revolution: Pennsylvanians in Arms and the Forging of American Identity* (University Park: Pennsylvania State University Press, 2004), chap. 3.

21. Knouff, *Soldiers' Revolution*, chap. 5; Spero, *Frontier Country*, chap. 10.

22. Quoted in Miller et al., *Irish Immigrants*, 570.

23. Gregory T. Knouff, "Soldiers and Violence on the Pennsylvania Frontier," in Frantz and Pencak, *Beyond Philadelphia*, 180.

24. Ibid., 188.

25. Patrick Griffin, *American Leviathan* (New York: Hill and Wang, 2007), 167–168; Knouff, *Soldiers' Revolution*, 155–157. For Williamson, see Ohio History Central, "David Williamson," accessed May 23, 2017, http://www.ohiohistorycentral.org/w/David_Williamson; for the possible identities of the men, including many with Scots Irish surnames, see George C. Williston, "The 1782 Volunteer Militia from Washington County, Pa and their Moravian Indian victims," accessed May 23, 2017, http://freepages.genealogy.rootsweb.ancestry.com/~gwilli824/moravian.html.

26. Knouff, *Soldiers' Revolution*, 182.

27. Spero, *Frontier Country*, 239–240, quote on 240.

28. Griffin, *American Leviathan*, 168.

29. Rob Harper, "Looking the Other Way: The Gnadenhutten Massacre and the Contextual Interpretation of Violence," *William and Mary Quarterly*, 3d. ser., 64, no. 3 (July 2007): 621–644; Spero, *Frontier Country*, 223–240.

30. Miller, et al., *Irish Immigrants*, 567–571, quote on 570–571.

31. Quoted in Knouff, *Soldiers' Revolution*, 245.

32. William Irvine to Ann Irvine, October 4, 1782, Irvine Papers, Historical Society of Pennsylvania, Philadelphia, PA, 7:22.

33. Margaret McFarland, Petition, April 21, 1787, Cumberland County, Pennsylvania, Orphan's Court, Docket Book 3:20.

34. Peter Gilmore and Kerby A. Miller, "Searching for 'Irish' Freedom—Settling for 'Scotch-Irish' Respectability: Southwestern Pennsylvania, 1780–1810," in *Ulster to America: The Scots-Irish Migration Experience, 1680–1830*, ed. Warren R. Hofstra (Knoxville: University of Tennessee Press, 2012), 165.

35. Kerby A. Miller, *Emigrants and Exiles: Ireland and the Irish Exodus to North America* (New York: Oxford University Press, 1985), 169; Maldwyn A. Jones, "Ulster Emigration, 1783–1815," in Green, *Essays in Scotch-Irish History*, 50; Miller et al., *Irish Immigrants*, 585.

36. Miller, *Emigrants and Exiles*, 169–171, 182; Miller et al., *Irish Immigrants*, 104, 287–288. See also Bric, *Ireland*, chap. 3.

37. Bric, *Ireland*, 206–213; David A. Wilson, *United Irishmen, United States: Immigrant Radicals in the Early Republic* (Ithaca, NY: Cornell University Press, 1998), chap 1.

38. For more on Mathew Carey and Irish America, see Nicholas M. Wolf and Benjamin Bankhurst, "Introduction: Mathew Carey and Dublin," *Eire-Ireland* 49, nos. 3 and 4 (Fall–Winter 2014): 172–175; Wolf and Bankhurst, "Introduction: Mathew Carey, Ireland, and the Politics of Transatlantic Debate," *Eire-Ireland* 50, nos. 3 and 4 (Fall–Winter 2015): 133–137.

39. Doyle, *Ireland, Irishmen*, 192.

40. Foster, *In Pursuit of Equal Liberty*, 129–130; Bric, *Ireland*, 216–249.

41. Pencak, "Promise of Revolution," 133, 140. For the 1790 constitution, see Pennsylvania Bar Association, "Pennsylvania's Constitution: A Brief History," accessed May 5, 2017, http://www.pabarcrc.org/history.asp.

42. James G. Leyburn, *The Scotch-Irish: A Social History* (Chapel Hill: University of North Carolina Press, 1962), 319.

43. Benjamin Rush quoted in Ridner, *Town In-Between*, 154.

44. Ibid., 156; see also 154–156, quote on 156.

45. Doyle, *Ireland, Irishmen*, 192–194; Miller et al., *Irish Immigrants*, 573; see also 536–546.

46. Ireland, *Religion, Ethnicity, and Politics*, 18–19, chap. 2; Foster, *In Pursuit of Equal Liberty*, 144–145. Foster identifies Samuel Bryan, not George, as the author of the *Centinel*. See also Doyle, *Ireland, Irishmen*, 194; Pencak, "Promise of Revolution, 142.

47. For a copy, see "The Address and Reasons of Dissent of the Minority of the Convention of the State of Pennsylvania to their Constituents," ExplorePAhistory.com, accessed May 26, 2017, http://explorepahistory.com/odocument.php?docId=1-4-15A.

48. Quoted in "Robert Whitehill Historical Marker," ExplorePAhistory.com, accessed May 26, 2017, http://explorepahistory.com/hmarker.php?markerId=1-A-279.

49. Ireland, *Religion, Ethnicity, and Politics*, 75–107.

50. Gilmore and Miller, "Searching for 'Irish' Freedom," 179; see also 165–181.

51. Griffin, *American Leviathan*, 225–233; Gilmore and Miller, "Searching for 'Irish' Freedom," 181–184; Thomas P. Slaughter, *The Whiskey Rebellion: Frontier Epilogue to the American Revolution* (New York: Oxford University Press, 1986), 3.

52. Slaughter, *Whiskey Rebellion*, 223–228; Spero, *Frontier Country*, 247–250.

53. Gilmore and Miller, "Searching for 'Irish' Freedom," 177.

54. Ibid., 168–170 (quote on 168), 177, 184–188.

55. Robert Davidson, *Sermon on the Freedom and Happiness of the United States of America, Preached in Carlisle, on the 5th Oct. 1794*, accessed May 25, 2017, http://deila.dickinson
.edu/cdm/ref/collection/ownwords/id/68.

Conclusion

1. Beverly C. Tomek, *Pennsylvania Hall: A "Legal Lynching" in the Shadow of the Liberty Bell* (New York: Oxford University Press, 2014).

2. Michael Feldberg, "Urbanization as a Cause of Violence: Philadelphia as a Test Case," in *The Peoples of Philadelphia: A History of Ethnic Groups and Lower-Class Life, 1790–1940*, ed. Allen F. Davis and Mark H. Haller (Philadelphia: Temple University Press, 1973), 56.

3. Zachary M. Schrag, "Nativist Riots of 1844," *The Encyclopedia of Greater Philadelphia*, accessed May 25, 2017, http://philadelphiaencyclopedia.org/archive/nativist-riots-of-1844/.

4. Emma Lapsansky, "Building Democratic Communities, 1800–1850," in *Pennsylvania: A History of the Commonwealth*, ed. Randall M. Miller and William Pencak (University Park: Pennsylvania State University Press, 2002), 157; for Philadelphia's population, see John K. Alexander, "The Philadelphia Numbers Game: An Analysis of Philadelphia's Eighteenth-Century Population," *Pennsylvania Magazine of History and Biography* 98, no. 3 (July 1974): 324. For western Pennsylvania, see Wayland F. Dunaway, *The Scotch-Irish of Colonial Pennsylvania* (Chapel Hill: University of North Carolina Press, 1944), chap. 5.

5. David Noel Doyle, *Ireland, Irishmen and Revolutionary America, 1760–1820* (Dublin: Mercier Press, 1981) 196–200, quote on 200.

6. Doyle, *Ireland, Irishmen*, 198; Lapsansky, "Building Democratic Communities," 161; David A. Wilson, *United Irishmen, United States: Immigrant Radicals in the Early Republic* (Ithaca, NY: Cornell University Press, 1998), 95, chap. 4.

7. Wilson, *United Irishmen*, 71, 62; see also chap. 3.

8. Ibid., 62–64; see also Liam Riordan, *Many Identities, One Nation: The Revolution and Its Legacy in the Mid-Atlantic* (Philadelphia: University of Pennsylvania Press, 2007), 213, chap. 6.

9. Wilson, *United Irishmen*, 72.

10. Lapsansky, "Building Democratic Communities," 161.

11. Ibid., 167.

12. Gary B. Nash, *First City: Philadelphia and the Forging of Historical Memory* (Philadelphia: University of Pennsylvania Press, 2002), 144 (quote), 157–158.

13. Ibid., 152–154.

14. Ibid., 147–152, quote on 147.

15. Kerby A. Miller, *Emigrants and Exiles: Ireland and the Irish Exodus to North America* (New York: Oxford University Press, 1985), 219; 204–205.

16. Wilson, *United Irishmen*, 90–93.

17. David Noel Doyle, "Scots Irish or Scotch-Irish," in *Making the Irish American: History and Heritage of the Irish in the United States*, ed. J. J. Lee and Marion R. Casey (New York: New York University Press, 2006), 152.

18. For the ethnic and racial breakdown of the state's population in 2015, see U.S. Census, "American Fact Finder: Selected Social Characteristics in the United States, 2011–2015 Community Survey 5-Year Estimates," accessed May 24, 2017, https://factfinder.census.gov/faces/tableservices/jsf/pages/productview.xhtml?fpt=table.

19. Synod of the Trinity, Presbyterian Church (USA), "History," accessed May 24, 2017, http://www.syntrinity.org/about/history/.

20. For the heraldry, see Daniel W. Patterson, *The True Image: Gravestone Art and the Culture of Scotch Irish Settlers in the Pennsylvania and Carolina Backcountry* (Chapel Hill: University of North Carolina Press, 2012), chaps. 4–5.

21. Michael Montgomery, *From Ulster to America: The Scotch-Irish Heritage of American English* (Belfast: Ulster Historical Foundation, 2007), 49–50. See also Alan Crozier, "The Scotch-Irish Influence on American English," *American Speech* 59, no. 4 (December 1984): 320–321.

22. Crozier, "Scotch-Irish Influence on American English," 318, 320, 326–327.

23. For "Greater Pennsylvania," see Carl Bridenbaugh, *Myths and Realities: Societies of the Colonial South* (Baton Rouge: Louisiana State University Press, 1952), 127 (quote) and chap. 3; Henry Glassie, *Pattern in the Material Folk Culture of the Eastern United States* (Philadelphia: University of Pennsylvania Press, 1968), 36–64, 195–196, 232–235. A bit less applicable but still informative is D. W. Meinig, *The Shaping of America: A Geographical Perspective on 500 Years of History* (New Haven, CT: Yale University Press, 1986), 131–144, 284–288, and 245 (map).

INDEX

JUDITH RIDNER is an Associate Professor of History at Mississippi State University and the author of *A Town In-Between: Carlisle, Pennsylvania, and the Early Mid-Atlantic Interior.*